McGraw-Hill's Statistics Discovery Series

A Guide to MINITAB

A Guide to MINITAB

Elizabeth Farber

Bucks County Community College

McGraw-Hill, Inc.

New York St. Louis San Francisco Auckland Bogotá Caracas Lisbon
London Madrid Mexico City Milan Montreal New Delhi
San Juan Singapore Sydney Tokyo Toronto

A Guide to MINITAB

This book is printed on recycled, acid-free paper containing 10% postconsumer waste.

1 2 3 4 5 6 7 8 9 0 DOC DOC 9 0 9 8 7 6 5 4

P/N 020209-5

The editors were Maggie Lanzillo and Jack Shira;
the production supervisor was Anthony DiBartolomeo.
R. R. Donnelley & Sons Company was printer and binder.

Library of Congress Cataloging-in-Publication Data

Farber, Elizabeth.
A guide to Minitab / Elizabeth Farber.
p. cm. — (McGraw-Hill's statistics discovery series)
Includes index.
1. Minitab. 2. Statistics—Data processing. 3. Mathematical statistics—Data processing. I. Title. II. Series.
QA276.4.F37 1995
519.5/0285'53—dc20 94-37781

Contents

Preface

MINITAB is a popular statistical software package that is widely used by colleges and universities as well as in business and industry. It is available on a wide variety of computer platforms including Macintosh, DOS and Windows. Its popularity can be directly attributed to the fact that its pull-down menus make it extremely easy to learn to use.

This manual is designed to complement any text in Elementary Statistics. The lessons in this text are self-explanatory so class time can be spent discussing statistical concepts while students can explore on their own with MINITAB. The MINITAB program relieves students of tedious statistical calculations and allows them to better understand statistical concepts presented in class.

Paralleling the development of a statistics course, this text takes two chapters to introduce students to using MINITAB. In subsequent chapters students explore various topics covered in class and in their main text. Problem sets are included at the end of each chapter that afford the opportunity for students to participate in simulations, analyze "what-if" scenarios and describe their findings containing MINITAB printouts. The printouts were obtained using the Windows platform but are similar to all versions. This manual comes with data disks formatted for DOS computers and for Macintosh. It it suggested that the files be copied onto student disks while the original files are kept intact.

Acknowledgments

Software was provided through the author's assistance program at Minitab Inc. in State College, Pennsylvania.

I'd like to thank Maggie Lanzillo at McGraw-Hill for her ideas and encouragement on this project. Thanks also to the many students who class tested the material found in this text and enthusiastically offered comments and suggestions. Many thanks to my sons Douglas and Michael, and to my husband Richard, for their love and support.

Elizabeth Farber

McGraw-Hill's Statistics Discovery Series

A Guide to MINITAB

I. Getting Started

MINITAB is a popular software program designed to take the drudgery out of statistics. Using MINITAB you'll perform lengthy computations, produce great graphics and create experimental simulations in a matter of seconds so you'll be better able to concentrate on the *ideas* and *concepts* presented in your statistics course. This manual will provide you with hands on activities and exercises and is intended to be used in combination with any basic statistics text.

When you've completed this chapter, you should be able to :

- Move about the MINITAB Data and Session windows.
- Enter data into a worksheet.
- Save a worksheet.
- Erase data.
- Generate random samples.
- Sort data.
- Tally data to get counts.
- Create an outfile.
- Retrieve a previously saved file.
- Manipulate columns of data.
- Display data in the Session window.
- Print an outfile.

Before you proceed, you'll need to know some basics. The MINITAB program is available for many computer environments and your professor or lab instructor can tell you how to first access the program. Copy the files from the Data Disk that comes with this manual on to a floppy disk.

*Notes*____

MOVING ABOUT THE MINITAB WINDOWS

The window you see when you open the MINITAB program depends on the platform you are working in. In this manual whenever there is a difference among the platforms, three versions will be shown. Naturally you need only refer to the one you are using so you might want to circle it as you go through this text.

MACINTOSH	DOS	WINDOWS
DATA WINDOW	**SESSION WINDOW**	**DATA WINDOW**

MINITAB actually works in several different windows at the same time. Although you may only see one window, the others are still at work in the background-out of sight just like a sheet of paper that's hidden by a second or third piece on top of it on your desk. Let's look at the two windows you'll use most frequently.

1. **The Session Window.** This window keeps a record of all the commands you give MINITAB and will display most of the output you request. When MINITAB was originally designed, it operated on its own command language that had to be memorized. Although these commands are still available and may be typed into the Session window any time you see the MTB > prompt, it is usually much more convenient to use the pull down menus appearing near the top of the screen.

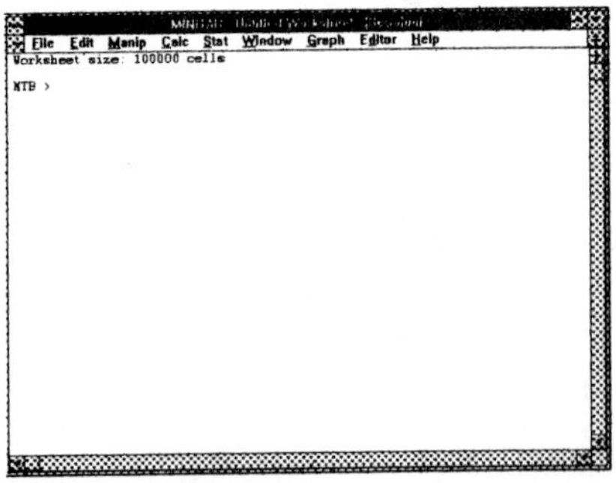

Session Window

2. **The Data Window**. This window looks like a spreadsheet and is composed of columns labeled C1, C2, C3 etc. and rows 1,2,3...It's where you'll enter your data values. You will usually want to enter values for a single variable in one column. The intersection of a row and a column is called a *cell* and there are many thousands of cells available to you.

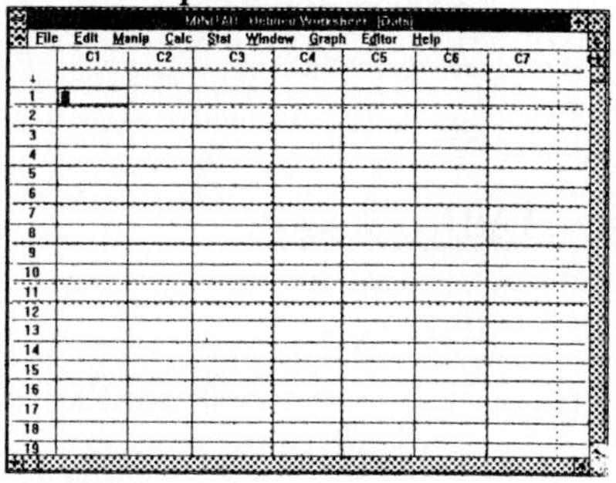

The method you'll use to access the Data Window pull down menus will also depend on the platform you're using. In the DOS version, you can access the pull down menu only from the Session window. In the other platforms the pull down menus are available from any window and appear near the top of the screen. To move back and forth between windows, do the following:

<u>MACINTOSH</u>

Use your mouse and point to Window in the pull down menu near the top of your screen . You'll see several options including **Session** and **Data.** Drag the mouse down to select the window of your choice then release it.

<u>DOS</u>

Hold down the **Alt** key and type **D** to get to the data window. **Alt-M** will get you to the Session window. To access the pull down windows you must be in the Session window.

<u>WINDOWS</u>

Use your mouse and point to Window in the pull down menu near the top of your screen . You'll see several options including **Session** and **Data.** Drag the mouse down and select the window of your choice then release the mouse.

*(With Windows you can also access the Data and Session windows by typing **Ctrl-D** and **Ctrl-M** respectively. For a Macintosh, you can hold down the propeller (Apple) key and type **D** for the Data window or **M** for the Session window.)*

Notes ____

ENTERING DATA:

Since MINITAB provides several ways to enter data, we'll look at various options. To do so we'll use the following data set that represents the first quarter weekly sales for each of two divisions of a large insurance company:

Week	Sales Division 1	Sales Division 2
1	10,283	10,874
2	12,283	28,316
3	14,291	3,917
4	17,392	19,291
5	9,826	31,927
6	10,293	6,291
7	11,837	26,191
8	10,382	8,171
9	8,271	3,182
10	11,927	1,032
11	12,917	9,120
12	10,271	2,135
13	12,903	1,823

Go to the **Data** window. The cell that is highlighted is the active cell and the values you type will go into this cell. Since you'll want to start by entering a 1 in the first row of the first column, be sure that this is the active cell. To move the active cell you can use your mouse and click on the cell or use an arrow key from your keyboard.

Type the numbers representing the week in column C1. Hit ↵**Enter** after you type each value or move one of the arrow keys. If you make a mistake at any time, just return to the cell, click on it and retype the correct value. Now enter the values for C2 and C3. It's important that when you do so you do *not* type a comma, a dollar sign or any symbol other than the ten digits 0 to 9, a decimal point or a minus sign. In the top row (in the DOS platform it's above the column numbers), type a name for each column. Use 'Week' for C1, 'Sales1' for C2 and 'Sales2' for C3. When you have finished entering the data, you'll want to save it since you'll use it again.

Hint: If your menu becomes "grayed out", try hitting ↵**Enter**. MINITAB *will not provide access to some commands if there is a pending value.*

SAVING DATA

Insert your formatted disk into the floppy disk drive. Then follow the directions for the platform you are using.

MACINTOSH

Point to the File menu, drag the mouse to **Save Worksheet as...** When you release the mouse a dialog box will appear. Click the appropriate buttons so your disk is in the active drive. Type Sales in the file name text box. To move about the boxes, point and click on the desired location or use your **Tab** key and move one box at a time.

DOS

From the Session window, choose the File menu . Hold down the **Alt** key and type the highlighted letter to select a menu. (In this case type **Alt-F**). Go to **Save Worksheet as....** Hit ↵**Enter** twice (since you'll be saving a MINITAB worksheet). The file name box will be highlighted. Hit the **Tab** key to highlight the files box and move the down arrow to [-A-]. Hit ↵**Enter**. **Tab** back to the

WINDOWS

Point to the File menu , drag the mouse to **Save Worksheet as...** When you release the mouse a dialog box will appear. Click the Drive arrow and highlight **a:**. Click **Select File** and click **OK.** Type Sales in the file name text box. You can move your mouse and click when you are in the right location or use your **Tab** key and move one box at a time.

file name box and type sales.
Type **Alt-O**.

The name of the file has now changed from 'Untitled Worksheet' to '1Sales.mtw". The extension .MTW is automatically added so that the computer can identify and read MINITAB files quickly. When you add more information to this file, use the **Save** option in the File menu . *It's a good practice to save your work often.*

Notes ____

____

OTHER WAYS TO ENTER DATA:

MINITAB's command language can be used to enter data. Go to the **Session Window** and notice the MTB > prompt. To enter data one ***column*** at a time type Set C4 after the MTB > prompt. After you hit ↵**Enter**, you'll see the Data > prompt on the next line. After the prompt type in the values for Sales in division 1. You can move to the next line any time you want by hitting ↵**Enter.** The Data > prompt will appear and you can continue typing the values. After the last value, hit ↵**Enter** and type End to restore the MTB > prompt. Your Session window will be similar to:

```
MTB > Set C4
DATA> 10283 12283 14291 17392  9826 10293 11837 10382
DATA> 8271 11927 12917 10271 12903
DATA> end
MTB >
```

To view your new entries, go to the Data window.

In some instances you'll want to enter your data by rows. To do so type Read after the MTB > prompt and specify the columns you want to use. As with the Set command, once you hit ↵**Enter,** the Data > prompt appears. At that time you can enter the data row by row as follows:

```
MTB > Read C5 C6
DATA> 10283    10874
DATA> 12283    28316
DATA> 14291     3917
DATA> 17392    19291
DATA>   9826    31927      [proceed until you get to the
                           last row.]
...
DATA> end
      13 rows read.        (Do not type this line)
```

MINITAB has a shortcut command for entering data that is in a sequence. Since you'll be using it often, let's see how it works by entering a column of values that number the weeks of the quarter.

MACINTOSH	DOS	WINDOWS
Point to the **Edit** menu and hold down the mouse.	Type **Alt-E** or point to the **Edit** menu and hold the mouse down.	Point to the **Calc** menu and hold the mouse down.

Drag the mouse down the pull-down menu to the line that reads **Set Patterned data** and release it. You will now see a dialog box that will help you communicate with MINITAB. Fill in the text boxes as requested. MINITAB allows you to name a new column directly in a dialog box. Simply type the name you choose inside the box following **Put data into column**. Use a name with 8 or fewer characters but do not type any spaces or the single ' quote. Since the name for each column in a worksheet must be unique, name the new column 'week2'. Move between the text boxes by using the **Tab** key or clicking your mouse on the desired location. Once the column name is specified, you'll want to **Start at** 1 and **End at** 13. Since you want to use the default increment of 1, you can simply hit the ↵**Enter** key and the numbers will be automatically listed. The Session window will record:

```
MTB > Name c7 = 'week2'
MTB > Set 'week2'
DATA>   1( 1 : 13 / 1 )1
DATA>   End.
MTB >
```

Examine the Session window output and note that the command **Name** is used to identify the designated column. (When you name a column or use a column name in a Session window command, you must use the single quotes.) The information inside the parentheses on the Data> line tells MINITAB to list the values starting at 1 and ending at 13 using an increment of 1. The value before the parentheses tells MINITAB to repeat the list 1 time and to repeat each value 1 time. Do not panic if this language is confusing. Remember that you can always instruct MINITAB to perform these commands through the dialog boxes available through the pull down menus.

You can form a variety of different patterns of data with this command.

★ **Example:** Enter the following values into column C10:
1 3 5 7 1 3 5 7 1 3 5 7 1 3 5 7

★ **Solution:** Use the **Set Patterned data** command from the pull down menu. **Start** at 1, **End** at 7 and use an **increment** of 2. **Repeat each value** 1 time and **repeat the list** 4 times.

★ **Example:** Form a column C11 with values:
5 5 10 10 15 15 20 20 25 25 30 30.

★ **Solution:** **Start** at 5, **End** at 30 and use an **increment** of 5. **Repeat each value** 2 times and **repeat the list** 1 time.

You'll also find this command handy when you need a long column with the same value in every row.

★ **Example:** Form a column named 'Rate' consisting of 300 entries of .065.

★ **Solution:** Click on **Arbitrary list of constants**. Type .065 in the **Constant** text box and 300 to **repeat the list**. The Session window equivalent is:

```
MTB > Name c11 = 'rate'
MTB > Set 'rate'
DATA>    300( .065 )1
DATA>    End.
MTB >
```

ERASING VALUES AND COLUMNS

To erase a single cell in the Data window, point to the cell and click to make it active. Then hit **Delete.** (In the DOS platform, hit **F10** then type **D**.) To erase an entire column, follow the directions given for the platform on which you are working.

MACINTOSH

Point to the **Calc** menu, hold the mouse down and highlight **Erase Variables...**. When the dialog box appears highlight C4-C8 then click on the **Select** button. (Double clicking the columns will also select them.) Click **OK** or hit ↵**Enter**.

DOS

From the Session window, choose the **Calc** menu (type **Alt-C**) and go to **Erase Variables...** Select C4-C8. Without a mouse, hit **F2** to get to the list box. Use the down arrow to get to a column and hit the **space bar** to highlight columns then hit **F2** select them. Type **Alt-O**.

WINDOWS

Point to the **Manip** menu. Highlight **Erase Variables...** When the dialog box appears highlight C4-C8 and then click on the **Select** button. (Double clicking the columns will also select them.) Click **OK** or hit ↵**Enter**.

To eliminate one or more *rows* of values, use the same menu but select **Delete Rows...**. Enter the appropriate information in the dialog box.

Go back to the Data window worksheet to check your results. Save the worksheet.

USING MINITAB TO FORM RANDOM SAMPLES

As you are learning in your Statistics class, generating random samples is of utmost importance. For this new activity, let's use a new worksheet. From the File menu select ...

MACINTOSH	DOS	WINDOWS
New Worksheet	**Restart** MINITAB	**New Worksheet**

Simple random samples are easy to generate with MINITAB. We'll look at two options: sampling without replacement (each member can only be selected one time) and sampling with replacement (where members can be selected any number of times).

★ **Example:** There are 573 students taking statistics at your college. Form a random sample consisting of 20 different students for a survey.

★ **Solution:** First form a column with a numeric values 1-573 to represent each member of the population. Naturally, you do not want to type all these values into a column, so use the **Set Patterned Data** command to form a column named 'Student' containing these numbers. Select the **Random Data** command on the Calc menu and then select **Sample from columns**. When the dialog box opens, you'll want to **Sample** 20 rows, **from** column C1 'Student' and **Put Samples** in 'Sample' .To do this, type 20, hit the **Tab** key, select (or double click) C1 'Student', hit the **Tab** key again and type Sample. Then click on **OK** (or type **Alt-O** on the DOS platform). Check the Data window of the new worksheet to verify that there is a new column with a sample of 20 values randomly selected from the population of values 1 to 573.

Notes ____

____

PUTTING YOUR DATA IN NUMERICAL ORDER:

MINITAB's **Sort** command will take selected columns of values and put them in either ascending (lowest to highest) or descending (highest to lowest) order. The **Sort** command can also alphabetize a column for you. Choose **Sort** from the appropriate menu.

MACINTOSH	DOS	WINDOWS
CALC	CALC	MANIP

The dialog box will ask you which columns you want to sort. Select C2 'Sample'. Then select C2 'Sample' for the column to **Put data into**. (This will rewrite the value into their original column. You can choose a new empty column if you wish.) You then must instruct MINITAB which column to use a criteria for sorting, so select C2 'Sample' for the **Sort by** box.. Later we'll see that when there are equal values, you can use a second column as a second criteria to sort by. In fact, MINITAB can sort up to four levels. Click **OK** (or type **Alt-O** for DOS users.) In the Data window you'll see the column with the sample numbers appearing in numerical order.

Repeat the exercises and form another sample of 20. **Name** the column 'Sample2' and **sort** the new sample.

If your sampling is done with replacement you can click on the **Sample with replacement** box.

★ **Example:** Select a sample of 20 from the 573 students, this time using the **Replace** subcommand.

★ **Solution:** Change the column you want to put samples in to 'Sample3' and select the "**with replacement**" option. Use the **Sort** Command to rewrite your column in numeric order. Did you get any repeated values? Form another sample of 20 with replacement and sort these values.

Notes ____

____

USING MINITAB TO SIMULATE AN EXPERIMENT

For the next activity. open a new worksheet. Go to the File menu and select:

MACINTOSH	DOS	WINDOWS
New Worksheet	**Restart** MINITAB	**New Worksheet**

★ **Example**: Flip a coin 100 times and record the outcomes.

★ **Solution**: Of course you could actually toss the coins, but its more fun to let MINITAB do the work. First type H in row 1and T in row 2. Notice in the Macintosh and Windows version, MINITAB adds -A to the column number. Columns that contain non-numeric alphabetic symbols (including a $, and %) are designated as *Alpha* columns and most of MINITAB's operations will not be accessible from these columns. To adjust for this, you'll need a *numeric* column so type 0 to represent Heads and 1 for Tails in a new column. Now have MINITAB perform the task of forming a random sample (with replacement) consisting of 100 rows of 0's and 1's. Put the sample in to a column you name 'Cointoss'.

COUNTING VALUES

Naturally you could count the number of 0's and 1's in your sample but MINITAB has a command that will do the task for you. Choose the Stat menu, then **Tables** and then **Tally.** Select 'Cointoss' for the variable. Click **OK** (**Alt-O** for DOS users). Your tallies will appear in the Session window.

Repeat the experiment and toss a coin 1000 times. Use **Tally** to count the number of o's (heads) and the number of 1's (tails).

PRINTING YOUR OUTPUT

When you do your assigned exercises, you'll want a "hard copy" of your results. You'll need a printer that is connected to your computer. For now, you'll see how to create a file that can print the Session window output. This file can later be imported to a word processing program and edited. From the File menu choose **Other Files** and then **Start Recording Session**. Hit ↵**Enter**. When you see the **Record Session As...** dialog box, you'll be asked to name the file. You'll want the file to be saved on your data disk, so be sure that the proper drive is selected. Type Chapter1 in the Filename text box. From the Data window it will appear that nothing has happened, but the in the Session window you'll see MTB > Outfile 'A:\Chapter1'.

From the time you start the outfile until you tell MINITAB to stop recording your session, every command you give and all the Session window output will be stored. At the end of this chapter, you'll learn how to print this record.

MINITAB also let's you annotate your file. To do so type # (the pound symbol accessed by holding down the Shift key and typing 3). Any text that follows will be included when you print your file. To see how this works, go to the Session window and type # This is an outfile created by YOURNAME. Hit ↵**Enter**

We'll continue with several more of MINITAB's capabilities in which you will produce some Session window output. At the end of this chapter, you'll print the 'Chapter1' file.

RETRIEVING A FILE

Let's go back to the Sales.MTW file and carry out some computations. To retrieve a previously saved file, go to the File menu and select **Open Worksheet.**

MACINTOSH

Click on **Drive** (or Desktop) to access the disk your data was stored on. Locate the disk name and click on it. Select **Open.**

DOS

Hit ↵**Enter** Then **Tab.** Use the down arrow to locate [-A-] in the files list. Hit ↵**Enter**. When the list of files from the A: drive appears, use the down arrow key to get to Sales.MTW and hit ↵**Enter**.

WINDOWS

Hit ↵**Enter**. Select drive **A:.** Click on Sales.MTW in the files list box.

MANIPULATING DATA

MINITAB has many built in statistical functions which we'll examine in later chapters, but very often you'll want to use it to do computations of your own.

★**Example**: Find the total value for the two divisions for each of the thirteen weeks in the quarter.

★**Solution**: From the Calc menu, select...

MACINTOSH	DOS	WINDOWS
Functions and Statistics then General Expressions	Functions and Statistics then General Expressions	Mathematical Expressions

In the dialog box, name the new variable 'total'. Then **Tab** down twice or point to and click on the **Expression** text box. To enter a formula, select (from the column list box) C2 'Sales 1' then type + and then select C3 'Sales 2'. When you click **OK** (or type **Alt-O** in the DOS version), MINITAB will form a new worksheet column in which the entry for each row represents the total sales for the two divisions.

Use the formula C2 'Sales 1'/ 'Total' * 100 to form a new column representing the percent of the total represented by C2 'Sales 1'. Name the new column 'Percent'. If you go to your Session window, you'll see. (Note that your column number may differ since MINITAB uses the next available column in your worksheet)

```
MTB > Name c13 = 'total'
MTB > Let 'total' = 'Sales1'+ 'Sales2'
MTB > Name c14 = 'percent'
MTB > Let 'percent' =  'Sales1'/ 'total'*100
```

The Session command for creating a formula is **Let.** For example if you want to take each value from C2, multiply it by 4, add the value 1234 and then subtract the square root of C1, go to the Session window and type Let C7 = 4*C2 + 1234 - sqrt (C1) after the MTB > prompt. (Sqrt will give you the square root.) Return to the Data window and verify that MINITAB formed a new column of values from the Session window command.

Since you have made changes in your file, save your file to include these changes.

DISPLAYING DATA FROM THE DATA WINDOW COLUMNS

MINITAB will not print directly from the Data window. Getting a "hard copy" of the quarterly sales data, will depend on the platform you are using. Choose the **Display Data** option from the indicated menu.

MACINTOSH	DOS	WINDOWS
EDIT	**EDIT**	**FILE**

Select C1 'Week' to C5 'Percent' and click **OK** (or type **Alt-O).** Your Session window will appear as follows:

```
MTB > Print 'Week' 'Sales1' 'Sales2' 'total' 'percent'.

 ROW   Week  Sales1  Sales2   total   percent

   1      1   10283   10874   21157   48.6033
   2      2   12283   28316   40599   30.2544
   3      3   14291    3917   18208   78.4875
   4      4   17392   19291   36683   47.4116
   5      5    9826   31927   41753   23.5336
   6      6   10293    6291   16584   62.0658
   7      7   11837   26191   38028   31.1271
   8      8   10382    8171   18553   55.9586
   9      9    8271    3182   11453   72.2169
  10     10   11927    1032   12959   92.0364
  11     11   12917    9120   22037   58.6151
  12     12   10271    2135   12406   82.7906
  13     13   12903    1823   14726   87.6205
```

Notice that the Session window command corresponding to Display Data is **Print.** You may prefer to use this directly from the Session window. At the next MTB > prompt type Print C1-C5 and hit ←**Enter.**

We've now completed the work for the Getting Started Chapter. In order to end the recording of your Session window, from the File menu, choose **Other Files**. Choose the option **Stop Recording Session**. In the Session window you'll see:

```
MTB > NoOutfile.
```

OBTAINING A HARD COPY OF YOUR OUTFILE

Your computer must be connected to a printer that has been properly selected. (Ask your lab instructor if you are having difficulty.)

MACINTOSH

From the File Menu choose **Print File** and select 'Chapter1.LIS'.

DOS

Choose Exit from the . File menu. Open a word processing program and import the 'A:\Chapter1.LIS' file. Print the file as you would any text file.

WINDOWS

From the File menu choose **Print Text File** and select 'Chapter1.LIS'.

(MINITAB adds a .LIS extension to its text files (outfiles)). The printout will list the annotations you have included after the # symbol, all commands issued, any errors you made and any Session window output. If you like, you can import this file to your word processing program where it can be cleaned up.

Notes

In the Macintosh and Windows versions, choose **Exit** from the File menu. **Save** your changes when requested to do so.

Exercises

1. Start to record your Session by creating an outfile named 'Chapter1.LIS'. In the Session window, type # YOURNAME after the MTB > prompt. For the last exercise of this chapter, you'll be asked to print this outfile.

2. A management consultant for Global Technologies has recorded the employee number and the number of billable hours for each of 50 employees during the previous week as follows:

Emp.#	Hours	Emp.#	Hours	Emp.#	Hours
670	38	705	51	187	47
561	25	363	50	607	50
828	38	721	37	873	47
580	40	969	51	570	46
153	44	955	48	964	47
127	43	849	48	442	43
484	42	929	37	420	56
798	40	951	44	898	44
519	64	250	49	705	37
422	46	410	57	443	38
433	36	571	54	953	32
770	49	505	32	962	41
711	38	265	42	187	43
576	44	504	47	884	58
216	30	399	46	169	38
453	42	742	55	167	43
779	41	730	35		

   a. Enter the data into C1 and C2 of a new file. Name C1 'EmpNum' and C2 'Hours'
   b. The hourly rate for each employee is $25. Calculate each employee's total gross salary. Put the results in 'Gross'.
   c. Each employee has a Federal Income Tax deduction of 18% of his or her salary. Calculate the deduction for each employee and store the results in 'withhold'.

d. Each employee has a social security deduction equal to 8.8% of his or her pay. Calculate the social security deduction for each employee. Put the results in 'FICA'.
e. The take home salary at Global is equal to the total gross salary minus the federal income tax deduction minus the social security deduction. Form a new column named 'Takehome' and calculate the take home pay for each employee.
f. Display C1-C5 in the Session window.
g. Save the file as 'Global.MTW'

3. The file '1Taxes.MTW' has been saved on the Data Disk from this manual. (If you have not yet done so, copy all the files on this disk to your own floppy disk.) The data comes from *Money* magazine and represents the taxes that would be paid by a hypothetical family of four living in each of the 50 states and the District of Columbia. In the study it was specified that the family income consisted of $72,385 in earnings, $2,782 in interest receipts, $455 in dividend and $1,472 in capital gains for a total of $77094. (Notice the alpha designation over C1 'State'.). Open this file.
   a. Sort the data into two new columns named 'State1' and 'Tax1' so that the data are listed in ascending order (from lowest to highest) by the amount of tax paid in each state. Since you'll want the state name carried along with the appropriate tax amount, be sure to select 'State' as well as 'tax' for your columns to be sorted.
   b. Compute the percent of total income paid in taxes for each state.
   c. Display the data in your Session window.
   d. Save the changes on 'Taxes1' on your own disk.

4. There are 548 students enrolled in the Management program at State University.
   a. Form a column named 'Student' that lists the integers 1 to 548.
   b. Form a simple random sample consisting of 25 different students (sample without replacement). Name the column 'Sample1'
   c. Sort the numbers in 'Sample1'.
   d. To form a systematic sample of 25 of these students, first have MINITAB select a number at random from one to 21. (Form a column with integers listed 1 to 21 then use the sample from columns command and use only one row.) Next have MINITAB form a column using the Set Pattered Data command and enter the data

into 'System'. Start with the number that was just randomly selected and list every 21st number.

e. Display your data in the Session window.

5. There are 157 restaurants listed in a local phone book. As a public health official, your job is to inspect the kitchens of 10 of them each week.
   a. Form a column with integers 1 to 157 listed.
   b. Obtain a random sample (without replacement) to select 10 restaurants in 'Check'.
   c. Sort the numbers in your sample.
   d. Display your data in the Session window.

6. Simulate the roll of a die 600 times.
   a. List values 1,2,3,4,5 and 6 in a column named 'Dice'
   b. Use Sample from columns (with replacement) to get a sample of 600 rolls in 'Roll'.
   c. Use the Tally command (under Tables in the Stat menu) to get a count of the number of times each value appeared.

7. Use the Set Patterned Data command to list the following values in C1 to C5. When you have finished, display your data in the Session window.
   a. 3 8 13 18 23 28 33 38 43 48 53 58 63
   b. 10 9 8 7 6 5 4 3 2 1
   c. 1 1 1 1 1 2 2 2 2 2 3 3 3 3 3 4 4 4 4 4
   d. 1 2 3 1 2 3 1 2 3 1 2 3 1 2 3 1 2 3 1 2 3
   e. 0.00 0.25 0.50 0.75 1.00 1.25 1.50 1.75 2.00 2.25 2.50 2.75 3.00

8. Stop Recording your Session. Print 'Chapter1.LIS' (your outfile). Do not worry if your mistakes have been recorded. In a later chapter you will learn how to delete unwanted output.

2. Up And Running

Now that you're acquainted with the MINITAB basics, let's take a look at some additional capabilities that will help you enjoy and understand your statistics course.

When you've completed this chapter, you should be able to :

- Compute statistics for columns of data
- Compute statistics for rows of data
- Store results as constants for later use
- Use the Edit Last Command shortcut
- Combine data from several columns into a single column
- Separate data from one column into several columns
- Copy all or part of a column
- Use the Help function
- Use the Info window

COMPUTING COLUMN STATISTICS

Open the '2Consult.MTW' file found on your Data Disk. This file represents the number of billable hours for each week of a five week management consulting project at Global Technologies. The entries in C1 are employee ID numbers and the rest of the columns list the number of hours worked by each employee for the specified week. Notice there are several cells containing *. This is the symbol MINITAB inserts for a missing value.

Usually all values of a single variable are listed in a column while different variables for the same case are listed by rows. Either way MINITAB makes it easy to compute many important statistics.

★ **Example:** Calculate the mean number of hours that employees worked for week 1.

★ **Solution:** The path for the command to compute various statistics for a column of figures varies among platforms. Point to the the pull down **Calc** menu and proceed as follows:

MACINTOSH	DOS	WINDOWS
DRAG TO FUNCTIONS AND STATISTICS AND THEN TO COLUMN STATISTICS.	DRAG TO FUNCTIONS AND STATISTICS AND THEN TO COLUMN STATISTICS.	DRAG TO COLUMN STATISTICS.

When the dialog box appears, you'll be given a choice of various statistics that can be obtained for a specified column. You're already familiar with many of them, and within several weeks, you'll be able to use them all. First compute the mean for C2 'Hours1'. Select ○ **Mean** and then select (or double-click on) C2 'Hours1' for the **Input variable**. When you hit ↵**Enter,** you'll see the result in the Session window:

```
MTB > Mean 'HOURS1'.
   MEAN      =       43.860
```

STORING VALUES AS CONSTANTS FOR LATER USE

If you are planning to use the value for additional computation or would like to print it out later, it's a good idea to store it. MINITAB provides 100 storage locations named k1, k2, k3...k100. The last few are reserved for special values such as π, but you can use any of the others. Select the option to store the result by clicking in the small square box. Then type k1 in the **Store result in...**box. You'll see:

```
MTB > Mean 'HOURS1' k1.
   MEAN     =       43.860
```

SAVING TIME USING THE LAST COMMAND DIALOG

Its easy to repeat the process for the other four weeks with a shortcut that MINITAB provides for using the same dialog box with a few changes. Use the combination of key strokes listed for your platform. (Hold down the first key as you strike the second.)

MACINTOSH	DOS	WINDOWS
APPLE-E	ALT-L	CTRL-E

It's only necessary to change the variable and the storage location for each column. Complete the process for the other four weeks and you'll see:

```
MTB > Mean 'HOURS2' k2.
   MEAN     =       44.780
MTB > Mean 'HOURS3' k3.
   MEAN     =       48.245
MTB > Mean 'HOURS4' k4.
   MEAN     =       43.750
MTB > Mean 'HOURS5' k5.
   MEAN     =       52.375
```

To obtain a list of these means type Print K1-K5 after the MTB > prompt as follows:

```
MTB > Print k1-k5
```

When you hit ↵**Enter,** you'll see the list of the five column means.

COMPUTING ROW STATISTICS

To find the mean for the number of hours worked by each of the 50 employees, you'll want to use the row statistics command. MINITAB will compute statistics for data listed in the same row when you specify the columns to be included. The results for any row statistic will be entered into a new column that runs parallel to the existing columns.

★ **Example:** Compute the mean number of hours worked each week by each employee.

★ **Solution:** Select **Row statistics** from the Calc menu. Select **Mean.** In the **Input variables** box, select C2-C6, the five columns containing employee hours. You'll want to name the newly created column to **Store the result in...**so type 'Empmean' in the appropriate box. Hit ↵**Enter**. From your Data window scroll to 'Empmean' where the mean of each of the 50 rows appears. It will be the next available column The commands in your Session window will look like:

```
MTB > Name c8 = 'empmean'
MTB > RMean 'HOURS1'-'HOURS5' 'empmean'.
```

COMBINING DATA FROM SEVERAL COLUMNS

★ **Example:** Find the sum of *all* hours worked on this project.

★ **Answer:** Of course you could use the column statistics command **Sum** for each of the six columns. But there's an easier way! First combine all six columns to a single column. To do this use **Stack** from the menu indicated.

MACINTOSH	DOS	WINDOWS
CALC	CALC	MANIP

Fill in each block with a column that will be in the stack. Select 'HOURS1' for the first block, 'HOURS2' for the second and so on. Type 'allhours' for the text box requesting the column into which you'll put the stack. You can use a subscript which will 'tag' the entries in the new stacked column in order to identify from which week they were entered. MINITAB will then number the columns to be placed in the stack. Select the **subscript** option and **Put subscripts into** 'Weeknumb'. Your Session window will look like:

```
     MTB > Name c9 = 'allhours' c10 = 'Weeknumb'
     MTB > Stack ('HOURS1') ('HOURS2') ('HOURS3')
('HOURS4') ('HOURS5') ('allhours');
     SUBC>   Subscripts 'Weeknumb'.
```

Notice the semicolon on the command line after 'allhours'. When MINITAB sees a semicolon it waits for a subcommand. MINITAB knows you are finished with your instructions when it sees a period. Now its simple to use the column statistic command to find the sum of all hours on this project.

```
     MTB > Sum
'HOURS5' k5.
          SUM      =
 2514.0
```

The hourly salary at Global is $25. To calculate the gross salary for each of the entries in 'allhours' , use the **Let** (Functions and Statistics) command. **Name** the new

> When you name a new column through a dialog box, it is usually not necessary to include the ' single quote marks. (An exception to this occurs if you wish to use a space or a special character in the name.) However, when a column is named in the Session window, the single quotes are essential. Throughout this manual we'll refer to named columns using the single quotes.

variable 'Gross' and enter 25*'allhours' in the **Expression** text box.

```
MTB > Name c11 = 'Gross'
MTB > Let 'Gross' = 25* 'allhours'
```

SEPARATING ENTRIES IN A COLUMN

Now we'll separate the entries in the 'Gross' column into weekly amounts. Remember the week has been identified in the 'Weeknumb' column. To do this, use the **Unstack** command found directly under the **Stack** command. In the first block type 'week1' in the second 'week2' until you have all five. You'll tell MINITAB to unstack the 'Gross' column using subscripts in 'Weeknumb'.

```
      MTB > Name c12 = 'week1' c13 = 'week2' c14 =
'week3' c15 = 'week4' c16 = 'week5'
      MTB > Unstack ('Gross') ('week1') ('week2')
('week3')    ('week4') ('week5');
      SUBC>   Subscripts 'Weeknumb'.
```

Go to your Data window to see the five new columns.

COPYING COLUMNS

To make each employee's gross pay easier to see, copy the entries in the first column to a column adjacent to 'week5'. The **Copy** command (Calc menu on a Macintosh and a DOS program or Manip menu for Windows) is useful for copying all or part of a specified column into a new column. Select **Copy** from the appropriate menu. Copy from C1 'empnum' into 'empnum2'. Although we'll be copying the entire column you can see options in the dialog box for either specifying rows to include or rows to omit.

```
MTB > Name c17 = 'EMPNUM2'
MTB > Copy 'EMPNUM' 'EMPNUM2'.
```

GETTING HELP AND INFORMATION

In addition to the help available from the pull down menus, there is another way to access help. You've probably notices a question mark in the lower left corner of each dialog box. To get help about any command, just click on the [?] symbol. If you look at the help available for the **Copy** command, you'll see some helpful suggestions on how to use it. Next time you have a question, try to use MINITAB's Help function before you try to hunt for your lab instructor.

Quite often when working on a large worksheet with rows and columns out of sight, you may forget various information you have stored. MINITAB has a function that helps you obtain important facts about the columns and constants that have been used. Obtaining information depends on the platform you are using, so instructions are given below.

MACINTOSH	DOS	WINDOWS
CHOOSE INFO FROM THE WINDOW MENU	CHOOSE GET WORKSHEET INFO FROM THE EDIT MENU.	CHOOSE INFO FROM THE WINDOW MENU

The following will be seen in your Session window.

```
MTB > Info.
```

MINITAB will report the name for each column you've used, how many entries and how many * are in each column. The constants used are also listed.

Notes ____

Exercises

Create an outfile named Chapter2.LIS to record your Session window output. After you have completed the assigned exercises, print your file.

1. Retrieve '2Consult.MTW' from your data disk. If the file has been changed , erase all variables except the original C1-C6. Calculate the median number of hours for employees in each of the five weeks. Store the values in constants. Use the print command (display data) to record these in your Session window.

2. Calculate the median number of hours worked by each employee. Place the results in a new column named 'Empmed'. Display the values for 'Empmed' in your Session window.

3. Calculate the mean for the hours worked by each employee and put the results in 'Empmean' .Display these values in your Session window.

4. Use the Let command to calculate the difference between 'Empmed' and 'Empmean'. Use the Print (Display data) command for the columns containing the mean, median and the difference of employee values. Write a brief paragraph to comment on the differences. What causes a large difference between the mean and the median?

5. Calculate the mode for week 1 using the tally command. Compare the mean, median and mode for this week. Comment on your findings.

6. Determine the maximum number of hours worked by an individual employee in week 3.

For 7- 14. Retrieve '2Stocks.MTW' from your data disk. The price of four different stocks has been recorded at Friday's closing each week for one year.

7. Compute the mean price for each of the four stocks.

8. Compute the median stock price for each stock.

9. Compute the mode for each stock.

10. The mean, median and mode for all four stocks are equal. As an investor, would you consider them all to be the same? Write a brief paragraph to discuss why.

11. Stack the stock prices from the four columns into a single column 'Allstock'. Use the subscripts subcommand.

12. Compute the mean, median and mode for 'Allstock'.

13. Separate the values into four columns.

14. Use the Info command to investigate the columns and constants used in your worksheet. List the columns that were used. How many entries in each? What constants were used?.

3. Descriptive Statistics

In this chapter you'll learn how to produce several types of graphical displays discussed in your text. In addition, you'll discover how easy it is to use MINITAB to compute all the descriptive statistics you are learning about in your course.

When you've completed this chapter, you should be able to :

- Produce histograms.
- Create frequency polygons and ojives.
- Produce stem-and-leaf displays, dotplots and boxplots.
- Obtain many basic statistics from a single command.
- Compute other descriptive measures.
- Produce histograms and boxplots in the Session window.

CREATING A HISTOGRAM

Open the '3Stocks.MTW' file from your Data Disk. Throughout this chapter you'll be using the data from this file to explore how to create various graphical displays presented in your main text.

★ **Example:** Produce a histogram of the 'Nutech' data.

★ **Solution:** Choose **Histogram** from the Graph menu and select the variable C2 'Nutech'. With no further instructions, MINITAB will make some decisions and produce a *default* histogram that will appear in a separate graph window. As you examine the default histogram, note that it consists of 8 classes, the class midpoints are 10, 15, 20...45 and the class width is 5.

If you prefer to create a histogram with a different number of classes or with midpoints other than those in the default display, MINITAB gives you the opportunity to issue subcommands from the Histogram dialog box so that you can design your own graph. Since there is a significant difference in options among the three platforms, we'll discuss each separately. As you did in earlier chapters, just follow instructions for the platform you are using.

Macintosh

You can select a first midpoint, a last midpoint or the class width by typing the value in the appropriate text box. Type 10 in the Interval width box and hit ↵**Enter.** To print your graph, choose Print window from the File menu.

DOS

You have the option to select a first midpoint, a last class midpoint or the class width by typing the value in the text box. Type 10 in the Interval width box and hit **Alt-O.** To print your graph, type **P.**

Windows

You can specify either class midpoints or cutpoints (boundaries). The easiest way is to form a new column in the Data window that contains the values for the midpoints (or cutpoints). To produce a histogram for C2 with class midpoints of 10, 20, 30, 40, 50, set these values into a new column named 'Midpoint'. Choose Histogram. Click on the Options box. Use 'Midpoint' to Define Interval values. To print, choose Print window from the File menu.

Now try different interval widths, midpoints (or cutpoints with Windows) for your histogram. Use the Histogram command again to produce a graph of 'Nutech' with 5 classes. Now try to obtain one with 12. Produce one with a first midpoint of 18.

CREATING A FREQUENCY POLYGON AND AN OJIVE

To create either a frequency polygon or an ogive you will need to provide two columns of information - the first to list the midpoint (class mark) for each class and the second to list the number of values in each class (frequencies). In order to have the polygon begin and end on the horizontal axis it will be necessary to include a midpoint for the class before and the class after the data. The frequencies for these classes will be 0.

★ **Example:** Create a frequency polygon for C2 'Nutech'.

★ **Solution:** First form a column with values 5, 10, 15, ...50 , naming it 'mdpt'. Then form a corresponding column 0, 1, 1, 3, 9, 20, 15, 2, 1, 0 (the values from the default histogram) and name it 'freq'. From the Graph menu follow the appropriate instructions:

Macintosh

Choose Scatter Plot. Select 'freq' for the Vertical axis and 'mdpt' for the horizontal axis. To connect the points, use the Lines option. Select 'freq' for the Y column and 'midpoint' for the X column. To print, select Print file from the File menu.

DOS

Choose Scatter Plot. Select 'freq' for the Vertical axis and 'mdpt' for the horizontal axis. To connect the points, use the Lines option. Select 'freq' for the Y column and 'midpoint' for the X column. To print, type P.

Windows

Choose Plot. Select 'freq' for Y and 'mdpt' for X. Use the Data Display drop down menu to select Connect. To print, select Print Window from the File menu.

An ojive (cumulative frequency polygon) can be constructed in a manner similar to the one used to construct a frequency polygon. Create a new column 'Cumufreq' in which the value in each row is obtained by adding the frequency of that row to those of the ones above it. The entries in the 'Cumufreq column will be 0, 1, 2, 5, 14, 34, 49, 51, 52, 52. Follow the directions for a frequency polygon, and use 'mdpt' for the X column, but use the column 'Cumufreq' in place of 'freq'.

CREATING EXPLORATORY DATA PRESENTATIONS

★ **Example:** Create a Stem-and-Leaf display for the Nutech data.

★ **Solution:** To obtain a Stem-and-Leaf display:

Macintosh	DOS	Windows
Choose Stem-and-Leaf from the **Graph** menu.	Choose Stem-and-Leaf from the **Graph** menu.	Choose EDA and then Stem-and-Leaf **Stat** menu.

Output	Comments
`MTB>Stem-and-Leaf 'Nutech'`	Session window command
Stem-and-leaf of Nutech N =52	*Reports the leaf unit.*
Leaf Unit = 1.0	

D	S	Leaf
1	1	2
2	1	5
2	1	
2	1	
4	2	01
6	2	23
8	2	45
14	2	667777
22	2	99999999
(7)	3	0000001
23	3	2222233333
13	3	455555
7	3	6667
3	3	
3	4	0
2	4	2
1	4	5

D= Depth S =Stems

In this default display, the leaf unit is 1 so the stem unit is 10. Note that there are 5 lines with a stem of 2 and 5lines with a stem of 3. The first line for a stem consists of values with leafs of 0 and 1-the second 2 and 3-the third 4 and 5 and so on. Reading down the depth column you'll see each row contains the total number of values in that row and in the ones above it. The line with parentheses contains the median There arc 7 values on this line. Reading from the bottom up, you'll see the total of the number of values for each row added to those below it until you reach the median.

Displays can be altered by adjusting the increment from the dialog box.

★ **Example:** Create a display of 'Nutech' which has 2 lines per stem.

★ **Solution:** Use the Edit Last command dialog shortcut and change the increment in the dialog box to 5. (Since the leaf unit is 1, the stem unit is 10. 10/2 =5.)

```
MTB > Stem-and-Leaf 'Nutech';
SUBC>   Increment 5.
```

```
Stem-and-leaf of Nutech N= 52
Leaf Unit = 1.0
   1     1 2
   2     1 5
   7     2 01234
  22     2 566777799999999
 (18)    3 000000122222333334
  12     3 555556667
   3     4 02
   1     4 5
```

For this display, the first line of a stem records the leafs with digits 0, 1, 2, 3 and 4 and the second line per stem records the rest. On the third line the 7 in the depths column means there are 7 data values on or above this line.

Finally, for a stem-and-leaf display with 1 line per stem, use an increment of 10.

```
MTB > Stem-and-Leaf 'Nutech';
SUBC>   Increment 10.
```

```
Stem-and-leaf of Nutech    N  = 52
Leaf Unit = 1.0

   2     1 25
  22     2 01234566777799999999
 (27)    3 000000122222333334555556667
   3     4 025
```

CREATING A DOTPLOT

The Dotplot command is also found in the Graph menu. If you are using Windows, first select Character graphs and then Dotplot. Create a dotplot for the C2 'Nutech' data. The display will be found in the Session window.

OBTAINING MANY BASIC STATISTICS WITH ONE COMMAND

MINITAB makes it easy to obtain several statistics for the same data set,. From the menu, choose Basic statistics and then Descriptive statistics. Select C1-C4. MINITAB will report 10 commonly used statistical measures for as many columns as you select. Your Session window will be similar to:

```
MTB > Describe 'Bluechip' 'Nutech' 'Amerbus' 'QCA'.

        N      MEAN    MEDIAN    TRMEAN     STDEV    SEMEAN
       52    30.212    30.000    30.217     1.696     0.235
       52    30.212    30.000    30.370     5.958     0.826
       52    30.212    30.000    30.370     6.746     0.935
       52    30.212    30.000    29.333     16.04     2.222

              MIN       MAX        Q1        Q3
Bluechip   27.000    33.000    29.000    32.000
Nutech     12.000    45.000    27.000    33.750
Amerbus     8.000    50.000    27.250    34.000
QCA         5.00     73.000    18.000    41.000
```

N is the number of non-missing values in the column, and you are already familiar with the MEAN and the MEDIAN. TRMEAN is the trimmed mean. It's useful when there are extreme values (outliers) in the column. The trimmed mean removes the top and the bottom 5% of the data and calculates the mean of the remaining 90%. . STDEV is the *sample* standard deviation. SEMEAN is the standard error of the mean. It's equal to the standard deviation divided by the square root of the sample size and its importance will be explained at a later time in the course. MIN and MAX report the highest and lowest values in a column and Q1 and Q3 give the first and third quartile.

If you examine the Session window output, you'll notice **MTB > Describe** followed by the column names. Type Describe C1-C4 after the MTB > prompt to see how it works. In the future we'll refer to this as the Describe command. In addition to the ten statistics it provides, the results of the Describe command are useful in computing additional statistics like the range, the interquartile range and the quartile deviation.

If the data in a column represents an entire population of values, the population standard deviation can be calculated by multiplying the sample standard deviation by the square root of (N-1)/N. For example, if the 'Nutech' data represented an entire population, the *population* standard deviation would be computed by:

$$\sigma = 5.958\sqrt{\frac{51}{52}} = 5.958(1.3937) = 8.3037$$

CREATING A BOXPLOT DISPLAY

Choose the Boxplot command from the following menu:

Macintosh	**DOS**	**Windows**
Graph	Graph	Stat Then choose EDA.

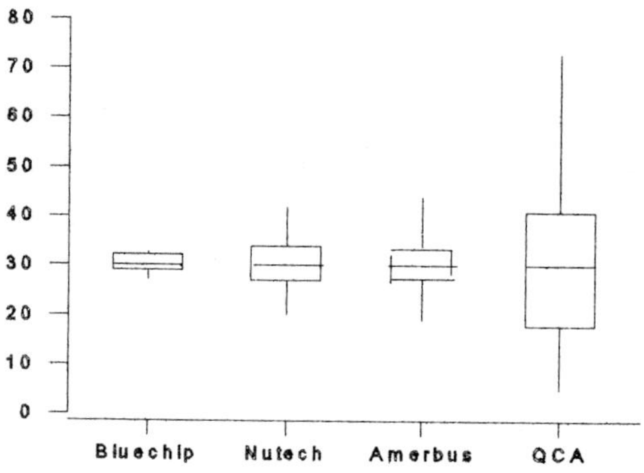

Boxplots are often used to compare distributions of several different variables. To compare the distributions of the four stocks, first stack all four columns into a single column called 'Allstock'. Be sure to use subscripts. Name the column containing them 'Subs'. Now select Boxplot. In the Macintosh and DOS versions, use the By variable option and enter 'subs' in the box. For the Windows version, enter 'Allstock' for Y and 'Subs' for X. The result is all four boxplots in the same window. You can see that for these data, the medians for the four stocks are equal but the distributions are vastly different.

PRODUCING GRAPHS IN THE SESSION WINDOW

MINITAB displays graphics in two modes-regular and high-resolution. Regular graphs are made up of keyboard characters and are displayed in the Session window. When a graphic requires High Resolution it will be found in its own separate graph window. Hi-Res graphs are made up of more *pixels* (picture elements) and are more attractive but require more time to construct and involve a separate command to print. The stem-and-leaf and the dotplot are by default character graphs. A histogram and a boxplot can optionally be displayed in the Session window as follows:

Macintosh	**DOS**	**Windows**
Click in the High Resolution box to de-select the High Resolution option.	De-select the High Resolution option by clicking in the box.	Choose Character graphs in the Graph menu and then choose the type desired.

★ **Example:** Produce a Session window histogram for 'Bluechip'.

★ **Solution:** Your Session window will look like:

```
Histogram of Bluechip   N = 52

Midpoint  Count
    27      2 **
    28      6 ******
    29     13 *************
    30      9 *********
    31      8 ********
    32      8 ********
    33      6 ******
```

Notes

Exercises

Create an outfile 'Chapter3.LIS' to produce your Session window output. Print the outfile as well as the Graph windows. Respond in paragraph form to each group of questions

1. The price of a LQ-95 Calculator in each of the 30 stores was as follows:

86	70	38	100	115	135	51	72	53	65
110	136	56	35	42	60	93	33	58	96
108	131	48	52	73	126	82	71	123	120

Open a new worksheet and enter the data in C1 'Price'.

a. Produce the default histogram for 'Price'. Then produce a histogram with 5 bars. Compare the histograms produced. Identify the class width for each. Discuss what happens to your description of the data set as you decrease the number of classes. What happens as you increase the number of classes?

b. Produce a stem and leaf display for 'Price' with a) one and with b)two lines per stem. Discuss which values represent the stems and which are the leaves. Use several values as examples. What is the leaf unit for each display ? The increment? What is the advantage this display over a histogram?

c. Produce a box-and-whisker display. Use the Describe command to identify the 5 key values.

d. Produce a Dotplot for the data.

2. Open the file '3Exerc.MTW' from your Data Disk. The data in C2 and C3 represent the price per share and the earnings per share for the companies in C1.

a. Produce the default histogram for 'Price/sh'.

b. Produce a frequency polygon for 'Price/sh' using the default histogram classes.

c. Create an ojive

d. Change the appropriate settings and produce a histogram with 5 classes.

e. Use the Describe command to produce 10 statistics
f. Form a boxplot for 'Price/sh'.
g. Produce a Dotplot for 'Price/sh'.

3. From '3Exerc.MTW', C4 and C5 represent the brand and the cost of scales rated by *Consumer Reports:*
   a. Produce the default histogram for 'Cost'.
   b. Produce a frequency polygon for 'Cost' using the default histogram classes.
   c. Create an ojive
   d. Change the appropriate settings and produce a histogram with 10 classes.
   e. Find the range, the interquartile range (IQR) and the quartile deviation QD using the output from the Describe command.
   f. Assume the data represents a population of values and compute the population standard deviation using output from the Describe command.
   g. Form a boxplot for 'Cost'.

4. In this problem you will explore the effects of extreme data values (outliers) on basic statistics. Assume the earnings per share of IBM increase to $250 while all other values remain the same. Use the Copy command to reproduce the data from 'Earn/sh' onto 'Earnsh2' and change the value for the IBM stock to $250.
   a. Use the Describe command to find the mean, median, minimum value, maximum value and sample standard deviation for 'Earn/sh' and 'Earnsh2'
   b. Compare the mean, median and standard deviation of the two columns. Which average was most affected: median or mean?
   c. How was the standard deviation affected?

5. In this problem you will multiply each data value by the same number to explore the effects on various statistics on the new data set. Enter the following data into C1 and name it 'Original'.

1 8 3 5 7 2 10 9 4 6 3

a. Create a new column C2 named 'Times10' where each data value from C1 is multiplied by 10.
b. Create a third column C3 named 'Times20' where each data value from C1 is multiplied by 20.
c. Use the Describe command and find the mean, median, maximum, minimum and standard deviation for C1-C3.
d. Compare the results in 'Original' with those in 'Times10' and 'Times20'. How do the means compare? How do the medians compare? How do the standard deviations compare?
e. Make an educated guess (a hypothesis) about what happens to the mean, median and standard deviation when you multiply each data value by the same number. Verify your guess by repeating the exercise and multiplying each value in C1 by 50.
f. How could you use the results of this exercise to simplify data entry for a data set with values .0025, .0037, .0062, .0053 and .0048?

6. Using the same worksheet as you did for the previous problem, you'll now investigate what happens as you *add* the same value to each member in the data set. Create a column 'Plus50' by adding C1 +50. Repeat for a new column 'Plus100' where each value represents C1 +100.
   a. Use the Describe command to find the mean, median, max, min and st. dev. for the three columns. ('Original', 'Plus50' and 'Plus100')
   b. Compare the mean, median and standard deviations of 'Original' with those in 'Plus50' ad 'Plus 100'. Which are the same? Which are different?
   c. Make an educated guess about how the mean, the median and the standard deviation are changed when the same amount is added to each data value. Test your hypothesis by predicting the values for the mean, median and sample standard deviation for data obtained by adding 75 to each data value in 'Original'.
   d. You need to compute the mean, median and the standard deviation for the data 23,752, 23,251, 23,735, 23,924 and 23,281. Explain how it is possible to simplify the data entry process.

4. Probability Concepts

In this chapter you'll explore the concepts of probability while you simulate probability experiments with MINITAB.

When you have completed this chapter, you will be able to :

- Simulate a probability experiment.
- Use the Tally command to count frequencies in a column.
- Sample from a specified distribution.
- Create a discrete probability distribution for a probability experiment.

SIMULATING PROBABILITY EXPERIMENTS

Performing probability experiments a large number of times can help you understand the underlying concepts of probability discussed in your class. Using MINITAB you can simulate experiments in a matter of seconds.

★ **Example:** Simulate the results of rolling a fair die 600 times.

★ **Solution**: First Enter the numerical outcomes 1, 2, 3, 4, 5 and 6 in C1 and **name** it 'Die'. (You can use the Set Patterned Data command if you like or simply type in the values.) From the Calc menu choose **Random Data** and then **Sample from Columns** .Type 600 rows to **Sample** and select 'Die' as the column to sample from. Type roll for the column to **store** the samples in.. Since values will be repeated, be sure to select the option to **Sample with replacement.**

The simulated results from 600 die rolls will appear in your Data window. From the Stat menu choose **Tables** then **Tally.** Since you'll want to summarize the frequency and the relative frequency of each of the 6 outcomes, select the **count** and the **percent** options. Your Session window will resemble:

```
MTB > Name c1 = 'die'
MTB > Set 'die'
DATA>   1( 1 : 6 / 1 )1
DATA>   End.
MTB > Name c2 = 'roll'
MTB > Sample 600 'die' 'roll';
SUBC>   Replace.
MTB > Tally 'roll';
SUBC>   Counts;
SUBC>   Percents.

     roll  COUNT PERCENT
        1     97   16.17
        2    107   17.83
        3     98   16.33
        4    103   17.17
        5    103   17.17
        6     92   15.33
       N=    600
```

In your statistics class you learned that each outcome has a probability of 1/6 to occur. How close did you come with your simulation? To get a quick picture of your sample results, create a Session window histogram for the 600 rolls. What shape is it?

```
Histogram of roll   N = 600
Each * represents 5 obs.
```

```
Midpoint  Count
   1    97 ********************
   2   107 **********************
   3    98 ********************
   4   103 *********************
   5   103 *********************
   6    92 *******************
```

SAMPLING FROM A SPECIFIED DISTRIBUTION

MINITAB can produce samples resulting from probability experiments involving random variables from many commonly occurring distributions. For now some of the names may seem strange, but you'll become familiar with many of them as you progress through your course.

★ **Example**: Generate a random sample consisting of 100 values selected from the set of digits 0, 1, 2, 3, 4, 5, 6, 7, 8 and 9. Obtain a list of all the values in your sample. When the sampling process is complete, use the **Tally** command with the counts and percents options to obtain a summary. Produce a histogram of your results and examine its shape.

★ **Solution**: This is an Integer distribution, so select **Random data** and **Integer** from the Calc menu. **Generate** 200 rows of data, **Store** the data in 'Digits' and specify a **minimum** value of 0 and a **maximum** of 9. Your Session window will be similar to the following:

```
MTB > Random 200 'Digits';
SUBC>   Integer 0 9.
MTB > Tally 'Digits';
SUBC>   Counts;
SUBC>   Percents.
```

To obtain a list of the data window values, use Display Data command. (You can also type Print 'Digits' in the Session window.)

MTB > Print 'Digits'.

The counts from one simulation will appear as follows (of course the one you obtain is bound to be slightly different).

```
Digits  COUNT  PERCENT
   0     23     11.50
   1     18      9.00
   2     29     14.50
   3     22     11.00
   4     22     11.00
   5     12      6.00
   6     21     10.50
   7     14      7.00
   8     18      9.00
   9     21     10.50
  N=    200

MTB > GStd.
MTB > Histogram 'Digits'.

Histogram of Digits   N = 200

Midpoint  Count
   0       23  ***********************
   1       18  ******************
   2       29  *****************************
   3       22  **********************
   4       22  **********************
   5       12  ************
   6       21  *********************
   7       14  **************
   8       18  ******************
   9       21  *********************
```

The results of this particular sampling vary only slightly from the uniform distribution we are sampling from in which all outcomes have an equal probability.

Sampling from a Discrete Probability Distribution

The previous example illustrated sampling from one type of discrete distribution, the Integer distribution. In the Integer distribution, every integer between the minimum and the maximum value has an equal chance of being selected. It's also possible to sample from other discrete probability distributions by providing MINITAB with two numeric columns of information-the first listing the numeric value of each possible outcome and the second listing its corresponding probability.

★ **Example**: Simulate obtaining the blood types from a sample of 1000 people chosen at random from the general population.

★ **Solution**: Enter the four basic blood types A, B, AB and O into C1 and name it 'Type'. Note that MINITAB affixes -A to the column number in the Macintosh and the Windows version to indicate this is now an Alpha column. Since MINITAB will not perform any simulations on Alpha (qualitative) data, it is necessary to create a "dummy variable" and express each outcome as a number. Use 1 =A, 2 = B, 3 =AB and 4 = 0, enter the numeric values 1, 2, 3 and 4 into C2 and name it 'Typenum'. Next enter the corresponding probabilities in C3 'Prob'. (.42 of the general population are type A, .10 are type B, .03 are type AB and .45 type O.) Note that this is a probability distribution since all the values fall between 0 and 1 and the sum of the values is 1.

To select a sample of 1000 people from the general population, select **Random data** from the Calc menu and then **Discrete. Generate** 1000 rows of data and **Store** in 'Blood'. Use the necessary values in 'Typenum' and the probabilities in 'Prob' . When you complete your selections, MINITAB will form a sample of 1000 blood types based on the given probability distribution. Use the percents option in the **Tally** command to see how close your sample came to the actual probabilities. Produce a histogram and examine its shape.

The values in your Data window will be:

ROW	Type	TypeNum	Prob
1	A	1	0.42
2	B	2	0.10
3	AB	3	0.03
4	O	4	0.45

And your Session window will resemble:

```
MTB > Name c4 = 'Blood'
MTB > Random 1000 'Blood';
SUBC>   Discrete 'TypeNum' 'Prob'.
MTB > Tally 'Blood';
SUBC>   Counts;
SUBC>   Percents.

  Blood  COUNT PERCENT
     1    432    43.20
     2    107    10.70
     3     28     2.80
     4    433    43.30
    N=   1000

Histogram of Blood   N = 1000
Each * represents 10 obs.

Midpoint  Count
     1     432  ********************************************
     2     107  ***********
     3      28  ***
     4     433  ********************************************
```

Exercises

Create an outfile named Chapter4.LIS to record your Session window output. After you have completed the assigned exercises, print your file. Use a new worksheet for each problem. Write a brief paragraph discussing the outcomes of each experiment.

1. Simulate tossing a coin 10 times and put the results in 'Toss10'. Repeat the experiment but this time simulate tossing a coin 100 times with the results going into 'Toss100'. Then do the simulation for 1000 tosses and finally 5000 times with the results going into 'Toss1000' and 'Toss5000'. Use the Tally command to examine the results for each of your samples. What happened to the percent of heads as your sample got larger?

2. Simulate the roll of a die 12 times using the Tally command to summarize the results. Did you get 2 rolls for each possible outcome? Now simulate the roll of a die 120 times and use the Tally command to calculate the percent of each outcome. Repeat and simulate the roll 1200 times. What conclusions can you draw from this experiment?

3. For this problem we'll use MINITAB to play "craps". In this game two dice are rolled and the sum of the faces is calculated. Set the values 1 to 6 into C1 'Die'.
   a. Simulate the roll of the first die by sampling 1200 rows from 'Die'. Store the sample in 'Roll1'.
   b. Next simulate the roll of the second die by sampling 1200 rows from 'Die' and storing the sample in 'Roll2'.
   c. Calculate the sum of the two rolls for each row and put the results in 'Sum'.
   d. Produce a histogram for 'Sum". What is its shape?
   e. Use the tally command to summarize the results of 'Sum'. Which sum had the highest frequency? Why?
   f. Are the results in 'Die2' independent of those in 'Die1'? Explain.

4. In the game "Plinko" on *The Price is Right,* a contestant drops the chip that randomly falls into a slot marked with a dollar designation. There are nine slots, 2 are marked \$0, 2 are marked \$100, 2 are marked \$500, 2 marked are marked \$1000 and 1 is marked \$5000.
   a. Set up two columns to represent the probability distribution for this game. (The outcomes of 0, 100, 500, 1000 and 5000 will be in one column and their respective probabilities in the other.)
   b. Simulate the results of 500 contestants playing this game. Store the sample results in 'Plinko'. Tally the results of 'Plinko" and produce a histogram for this column.
   c. Calculate the mean of 'Plinko' to determine the average of the amounts won by each of the 500 contestants. Compute the expected value using the formula from your text. How close did the results of your simulation come?

5. Probability Distributions

In this chapter you'll explore several of the probability distributions that are essential to your study of inferential statistics.

When you complete this chapter you will be able to:

- Simulate probability experiments.
- Obtain probabilities from specific distributions.
- Find the value of random variable value given specific probability conditions.

SIMULATING BINOMIAL EXPERIMENTS

Imagine taking a 5 question multiple choice quiz in which each question has 4 choices but since you do not have any information about the subject matter, each answer is a random guess. This is of course a binomial experiment for which n = 5, p =.25 and q = .75. Now suppose 1000 students (without any more information than you had) take the same quiz and the number of questions correctly answered by each is calculated.

★ **Example:** Simulate the experiment just described.

★ **Solution:** Choose **Random data** from the Calc menu and choose **Binomial** from the distribution list. **Generate** 1000 rows of data and **Store in** 'Correct'. The **number of trials** is 5 and the **probability of success** is .25. In a matter of seconds MINITAB will grade each of the 1000 tests by counting the number of correct responses on each one. The record will be kept in 'Correct'.

Once the results are entered in the Data window, use the **Tally** command under **Tables** in the Stat menu to quickly look at the distribution of scores. Select all the display options for the **Tally** command so you can get a report on the count for each score, the percent of students who got this score, the cumulative count and the cumulative probability.

Your Session window will resemble:

```
MTB > Name c1 = 'correct'
MTB > Random 1000 'correct';
SUBC>   Binomial 5 .25.

MTB > Tally 'correct';
SUBC>   Counts;
SUBC>   Percents;
SUBC>   CumCounts;
SUBC>   CumPercents.
 correct  COUNT PERCENT CUMCNT  CUMPCT
       0    229   22.90    229   22.90
       1    379   37.90    608   60.80
       2    279   27.90    887   88.70
       3     99    9.90    986   98.60
       4     12    1.20    998   99.80
       5      2    0.20   1000  100.00
      N=   1000
```

Construct a histogram to describe the outcomes of this binomial experiment. (In Windows you can select a percent histogram under Options.)

From your text you know the expected value for this experiment is $\mu = np = 5(.25) = 1.25$. That is if an infinite number of students took this quiz under the same conditions, the average number of questions correct would be 1.25. The standard deviation would be .968. Use the **Describe** command to compute the mean and the standard deviation for 'Correct' and compare it with the population parameters obtained from using formulas.

$$\sqrt{npq} = \sqrt{5(.25).75)} = \sqrt{.9375} = .968$$

```
MTB > Describe 'correct'.
```

N	MEAN	MEDIAN	TRMEAN	STDEV	SEMEAN
1000	1.2620	1.0000	1.2511	0.9696	0.0307

MIN	MAX	Q1	Q3
0.0000	5.0000	1.0000	2.0000

*notes*____

____

OBTAINING BINOMIAL DISTRIBUTION PROBABILITIES

★ **Example:** What is the probability of getting exactly 3 questions correct on the quiz just described?

★ **Solution:** In your statistics class you have discussed the options of using a formula or a binomial table to calculate the solution. Both of these methods have limitations so we'll now see how to use MINITAB to perform probability calculations.

Construct the probability distribution using two columns. Since this is a *discrete* distribution **Set** all the possible random variable values (0, 1, 2, 3, 4, 5) in the first column and name it 'x'. To obtain the corresponding probability values, choose the **Probability Distribution** command from the **Calc** **menu**. As in the Random Data command, you will see many distributions listed, but for now we'll concentrate on the **Binomial** so choose it from the list. Note that when the dialog box opens you'll see three options at the top:

- O **Probability**
- O **Cumulative probability**
- O **Inverse cumulative probability**

The options will be the same for whatever distribution you choose from the list, however the parameters needed to perform calculations will differ from one distribution to another. For a binomial distribution, you'll be asked to provide the values for n and p. We'll use n = 5 and p = .25 for this example.

Be sure the ● **Probability** option is highlighted at the top of the dialog box. Select the **Input column** button and select 'x' for its text box. Type PDF in the **optional storage** text box. Go to the Data window to see the values. (Without the optional storage, the information will be placed in the Session window but will not be stored.) Each value in the 'PDF' column represents the height of the probability histogram at the x value found in the same row. Recall that the area of a rectangle is equal to its width times its height and since the width of each bar is one unit, the area of each bar in the histogram is equal to its height. For a discrete distribution, the PDF value corresponds to the probability that the outcome of an experiment will be *exactly* equal to x.

Now let's examine the Cumulative probability option. Return to the **Probability distribution** dialog box and select ● **Cumulative probability** at the top. The values of n and p will remain the same as will the **Input column,** 'x'. Change the **Optional storage** to 'CDF'. and click OK. If you **Display the data** in the three columns, you'll have a Session window output of:

ROW	x	PDF	CDF
1	0	0.237305	0.23730
2	1	0.395508	0.63281
3	2	0.263672	0.89648
4	3	0.087891	0.98437
5	4	0.014648	0.99902
6	5	0.000977	1.00000

Note that PDF3 means the probability that x=3 whereas CDF 3 means the probability that x ≤ 3.Compare the values listed in 'PDF' and 'CDF'. Note that the values in row 1 are `0.23730` for both columns. In the second row .395508 is the probability of answering *exactly one* question correct and .63281 is the probability of answering *one or fewer* correct. Verify that the second row entry of 'CDF' (0.63281) represents the sum of the values 0.237305+ 0.395508 found in 'PDF' in rows 1 and 2. And the third row in 'CDF' is the sum of the first three rows in 'PDF'. As you would suspect, the last entry in the 'CDF' column is always 1.

★ **Example:** What is the probability of:

a) Answering 3 or less questions correctly?

b) Answering at least 2 questions correctly?

c) of answering between 2 and 4 (including 2 and 4) correctly?

★ **Solutions:**

a) To calculate the probability of answering 3 or less question correctly you could, of course, add the values in 'PDF' corresponding to the values for x = 0, 1, 2, and 3. However, it's much simpler to use the 'CDF' value for x = 3 to find there's a 0.89648 probability of answering 3 or less questions correctly.

b) To find the probability of getting at least 2 questions correct (2 or 3 or 4 or 5), use 0.63281 the value in the 'CDF' column for x = 1 to add the probability of getting 0 or 1 questions correct. Subtract this from 1 to obtain the probability of the complement (getting 2 or 3 or 4 or 5 correct). 1 - 0.63281 = .36719.

c) To calculate the probability of getting between 2 and 4 solutions (including 2 and 4) correct, use the 'CDF' for x = 4 (0.99902) to obtain the total of probabilities for x = 0, 1, 2, 3, and 4. Then subtract 0.63281 the 'CDF' value for x = 1. The probability that x = 2 or 3 or 4 is 0.99902- 0.63281 = .36621 .

For a small value of n such as n =5 in our example, the use of the Cumulative probability cannot be fully appreciated, so let's look at another problem.

★ **Example:** In a Gallup poll, 53 percent of the eligible women responding said they would not date a co-worker. If 100 employed women are selected at random and asked if they would data a co-worker what is the probability that:

a) 50 or fewer would date a co-worker?
b) At least 40 would date a co-worker?
c) Between 45 and 60 (including 45 and 60) would date a co-worker?

★ **Solutions:** Select **Probability Distributions** and then **Binomial** from the Calc menu. Select **Cumulative probability** and type 100 for the number of trials and .53 for the probability of success. Select the **Input constant** option since you'll only need a few 'CDF' values. Do not select optional storage so your output will appear in the Session window.

a) Type 50 in the **Input constant** box. The Session window will report:

```
MTB > 'CDF' 50;
SUBC>    Binomial 100 .53.
           K  P( X LESS OR = K)
     50.00                0.3078
```

CDF 50 =.3078 means that the probability that x is less than or equal to 50 is .3078.

b) First calculate the probability that x is 39 or less using the Cumulative distribution input constant 39.

```
MTB > 'CDF' 39;
SUBC>    Binomial 100 .53.
           K  P( X LESS OR = K)
     39.00                0.0034
```

Subtract this value from 1 to obtain your solution. (Use a calculator or MINITAB'S **Let** command. Recall that to view the computation, use the Print command.)

```
MTB > LET K1 = 1-.0034
```

```
MTB > PRINT K1
K1        0.996600
```

The probability at least 40 will data a co-worker is .996600.

c) First calculate the 'CDF' for 60 to add the probabilities that x = 0, 1, 2,...60. Then subtract 'CDF' for 44 (the probability x = 0, 1, 2,...44.) This of course will leave the probabilities for x = 45 to 60. If you use K1 to for the first optional storage location and K2 for the second, you can compute and view your solution in the Session window using the * Let and ** Print command as follows. (Of course you could also use a handy calculator for the same result.)

```
MTB > 'CDF' 60 k1;
SUBC>   Binomial 100 .53.
MTB > 'CDF' 44 k2;
SUBC>   Binomial 100 .53.
MTB > Let k3 = k1 -k2      *
MTB > Print k3            **

K3        0.889695
```

There's close to a .89 probability that between 45 and 60 eligible women would date a co-worker.

SIMULATING POISSON EXPERIMENTS

The Poisson distribution is another commonly applied discrete probability distribution. Simulations are similar to those done for binomial experiments.

★ **Example:** An average of three cars arrive at a highway tollgate every minute. This rate is approximated by a Poisson distribution. Simulate the count of the number of cars arriving each minute during an 8 hour shift (240 minutes).

★ **Solution:** Choose **Random data** and then **Poisson** from the Calc menu. **Generate** 240 rows and **Store** in 'Cars'. The only parameter you'll need to provide is 3 for the mean.

Choose the **Tally** command under **Tables** in the Stat menu to examine at the distribution of counts. Select all the options for the **Tally** command so you can obtain the count for each value, the percent of time periods this number of cars arrived at the tollgate, the cumulative count and the cumulative probability.

Construct a **histogram** to describe the outcome of this Poisson experiment.

Compute the mean for 'Cars' and compare it to the given mean. Next compute the variance (square the standard deviation) for your Poisson sample. In a Poisson distribution, the population mean is equal to the population variance. How close did your sample values come?

COMPUTING POISSON PROBABILITIES

★ **Examples:** What is the probability that exactly 4 cars will arrive in a minute? What is the probability that at least 2 cars will arrive in a minute? These questions and others can be answered using the **Probability distribution** in the Calc menu and choosing **Poisson** from the list. As before provide 3 for the mean.

★ **Solutions:** To determine the probability that exactly 4 cars will arrive in a minute select the **Probability** option and use 4 as the **Input constant**.

```
MTB >  PDF 4;
SUBC>   Poisson 3.
       K           P( X = K)
     4.00             0.1680
```

The probability exactly 4 cars will arrive in a minute is .1680.

To find the probability at least 2 cars will arrive in a minute select Cumulative probability and use an **Input constant** of 1. When you get the result, subtract it from 1.

```
MTB > 'CDF' 1;
SUBC>    Poisson 3.
           K  P( X LESS OR = K)
        1.00               0.1991
MTB > let k1 = 1-.1991
```
(*You might prefer to use a calculator here.*)
```
MTB > Print k1

K1         0.800900
```

The probability that at least 2 cars will arrive in a minute is about .80

SIMULATING A NORMAL DISTRIBUTION EXPERIMENT

The previous problems involved discrete random variables. As you learned in your statistics class, the normal distribution is an example of a continuous random variable. Let's now look at a simulation involving this continuous distribution.

★ **Example:** In a study of depressed patients, it was found that the age at onset of depression for those in dysfunctional families was normally distributed with a mean and standard deviation of 30.6 years and 9.1 years respectively. Simulate the age of onset of depression for 200 patients.

★ **Solution:** From the Calc menu choose **Random data** and then **Normal** in the distribution list. **Generate** 200 rows of data and **Store** in 'Onset'. Enter the mean and standard deviation parameters 30.6 and 9.1. When your sample is displayed in the Data window, notice that the values are not integers but rather can be any real number. This is a critical difference between a discrete distribution (like the integer, binomial or Poisson) and a continuous distribution. Since the **Tally** command is for discrete data, it is not too useful here since you *probably* have 200 *different* values from your simulation. Produce a histogram of your 'Onset' simulation results and examine the shape. Compute the mean and the standard deviation for your 'Onset' sample and compare them to the given population values.

```
MTB > Name c1 = 'onset'
MTB > Random 200 'onset';
SUBC>   Normal 30.6 9.1.
MTB > Mean 'onset'.
   MEAN      =        30.456
MTB > StDev 'onset'.
   ST.DEV. =          9.0032
MTB > Histogram 'onset'
```

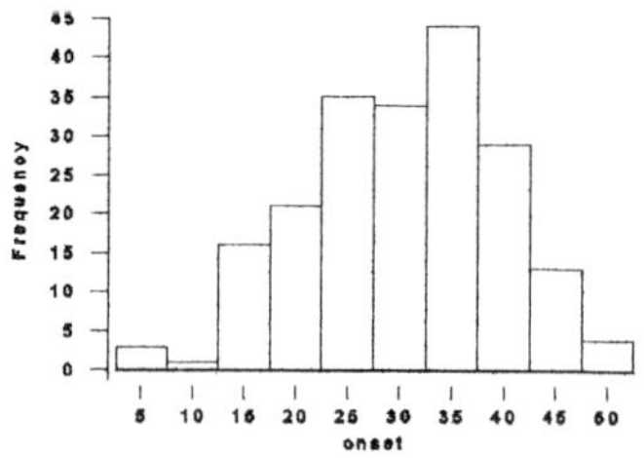

COMPUTING NORMAL DISTRIBUTION PROBABILITIES

Although we could never list *all* the values possible for a continuous distribution, we'll illustrate the shape of the normal distribution using some values from the standard normal curve (the default at mean = 0 and sigma = 1). Choose the **Set Patterned data** command and **Put data** values into 'zscore' Since almost all the values will fall between -3.5 and +3.5 we'll **Start at** -3.5 and **End at** 3.5. Use an **Increment** of .05.

From the Calc menu choose **Probability Distribution** and then **Normal**. Select the **Probability density** function (top button) and use the default mean and standard deviation. Select 'zscore' for the **Input column** and designate 'PDF' for the **Optional storage**. Once the 'PDF' column is formed, construct a **scatter plot** using 'PDF' for the **Vertical axis (Y variable)** and 'zscore' for the **Horizontal axis (X variable).** Connect the points.

You should now see a drawing of the standard normal curve in a graph window. For a continuous distribution, the Probability density function (PDF) supplies the value for the height of the curve at the specified value of x. (As you know, the probability that a continuous random variable x is exactly equal to a given value is virtually zero i.e.
P(x = 2.0654321) = 0.)
Therefore, for a continuous distribution, it is only meaningful to compute the probability that x (or z in the case of the standard normal curve) falls *within an interval*.

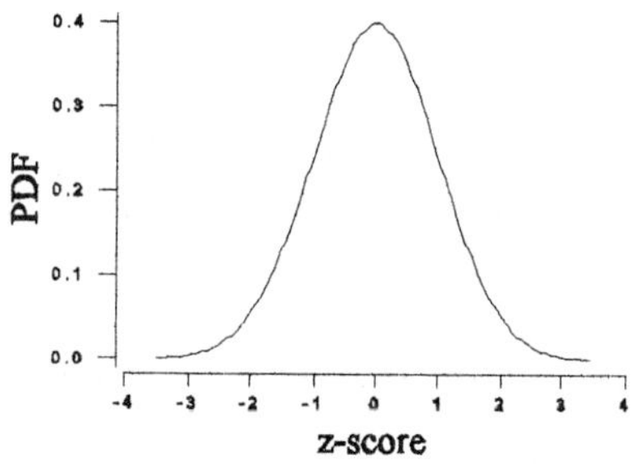

Let's now see how the Cumulative density function (which gives the proportion of area falling under the curve and to the *left* of the vertical line drawn at the input value) works for the normal distribution. Return to the **Normal distribution** dialog box and select the **Cumulative density** function button. Use the default values for the mean and standard deviation, 'zscore' for the **Input column** and type 'cumuprob' to name the **Optional storage** column.

Go to the Data window to view the output and note that the first few values in 'cumuprob' are very close to zero. Scroll down the column and verify that the values increase to nearly 1 on the last row. Note that on row 141 where 'zscore' = 0, the Cumulative density is .5000 (why?).

★ **Examples:** Return to the study about the age of onset for depression. Recall that the mean and standard deviation were given as 30.6 and 9.1 years.

a)What is the probability that the age of onset of depression is less than 30?

b)What is the probability that the age of onset of depression is at least 40?
c)What is the probability the age is between 25 and 35.

★ **Solutions:** Each of the previous questions can be answered with the Cumulative density function command and perhaps some additional elementary computation. Select the **Probability distribution** command and **Normal** from the distribution list. Type the parameters 30.6 for the mean and 9.1 for the standard deviation. Select the Input constant button but the optional storage is only helpful if you intend to do your arithmetic computations on MINITAB.

a) Type 30 for the **Input constant**. The Session window output will resemble:

```
MTB > CDF 30;
SUBC>    Normal 30.6 9.1.
   30.0000     0.4737
```

The probability the age of onset is less than 30 is .4737.

b) Use 40 for the input constant to obtain the probability the age of onset is *less than* 40.

```
MTB > CDF 40;
SUBC>    Normal 30.6 9.1.
   40.0000     0.8492
MTB > let k5 = 1-.8492
MTB > print k5
K5        0.150800
```

After subtracting the output from 1, we find .1508 is the probability the age of onset is at least 40. (Note that since the probability the age is *exactly equal* to 40 is virtually 0, we can use probabilities for "less than" and "less than or equal to" interchangeably in a continuous distribution.)

c) We'll need two cumulative probabilities for this question. First compute the larger value using 35 as the **Input constant,** then return to the dialog box and specify 25 for the **Input constant**. The solution is the first value minus the second. If you store the output in constants k10 and k11, your Session window will look like:

```
MTB > CDF 35 k10;
SUBC>   Normal 30.6 9.1.
MTB > CDF 25 k11;
SUBC>   Normal 30.6 9.1.
MTB > let k12 = k10 -k11
MTB > print k12
K12       0.416485
```

The probability the age of onset is between 25 and 35 is .4165.

FINDING RANDOM VARIABLE VALUES GIVEN SPECIFIED PROBABILITIES

For the Cumulative density function, we use a value of the random variable as input while the output is the area falling to the left of this value under the normal curve. Since this is a one-to-one function, as you learned in your algebra class, it has an inverse. We'll now examine the Inverse cumulative probability function.

When we have a specified cumulative area (probability) and want to know the random variable value such that this area is to it's left under the normal distribution curve, we'll use the Inverse cumulative density function.

★ **Examples:** Here are some examples using the standard normal curve for which this inverse function can be put to use.

a) Find the z-score such that 5% of area lies to its left.

b)Find the z-score such that 90% of the area lies to its right.

c) Find values for -z and +z such that 99% of area under the curve falls between these standard scores.

★ **Solutions:** Select **Probability Distributions** and **Normal** from the **Calc** menu. Select the **Inverse cumulative probability** button and use the default mean = 0 and standard deviation =1. Your **Input constant** will be the area that would be falling to the *left* of the unknown z-score. The Session window output will be the required z-score value.

a) The **Input constant** is .05. The Session window will report:

```
MTB > InvCDF .05;
SUBC>    Normal 0.0 1.0.
    0.0500   -1.6449
```

The required z-score is -1.6449

b) **Input constant** is .10 (computed by 1-.90).

```
MTB > InvCDF .10;
SUBC>    Normal 0.0 1.0.
    0.1000   -1.2816
```

The z-score is -1.2816

c) The **Input constants** are .005 and .995. (computed from ½(1-.99) and ½(1+.99).

```
MTB > InvCDF .005;
SUBC>    Normal 0.0 1.0.
    0.0050   -2.5758
MTB > InvCDF .995;
SUBC>    Normal 0.0 1.0.
    0.9950    2.5758
```

The z scores are ± 2.5758. (Although we worked with two-scores, note that it's only necessary to compute one-the other is its opposite.)

The Inverse cumulative probability is also useful in answering questions such as:

★ **Examples:** Scores for a particular civil service exam are normally distributed with a mean of 137 points and a standard deviation of 17.2 points. Applicants for civil service jobs must take this test, and the top 10% can be offered jobs. What is the cut-off score that separates the highest 10% of the test scores from the others?

★ **Solutions:** Select **Probability Distributions** then **Normal** from the Calc menu. Select the **Inverse cumulative probability** button and type in 137 for the mean and 17.2 for the standard deviation. The **Input constant** is .90 (1-.10). The Session window result is

```
MTB > InvCDF .90;
SUBC>   Normal 137 17.2.
    0.9000  159.0427
```

The score that separates the top 10% from the lower 90% is 159.0427. Persons scoring at least 160 can be offered a job.

*Notes*____

Exercises

Create an outfile Chapter6.LIS for this set of problems and use Session window histograms. Print your outfile and solution each question with a brief paragraph.

1. A recent study found that of the patients receiving heart transplants after 1983, 83% were still alive.
   a. A physician randomly selects 6 patients who received heart transplants after 1983 and determines the number who are still alive. Suppose this binomial experiment were to be repeated 500 times. Create a simulation for this and store the results in 'Alive'. Use the Tally command to summarize the outcomes in 'Alive'.
   b. Produce a histogram of 'Alive'.
   c. Use the Describe command to determine the mean and the standard deviation for 'Alive'. How does this compare with the theoretical mean and standard deviation computed by using formulas found in your text. Comment on the difference.

2. In a poll conducted by the Olsten Corporation, a temporary personnel firm, 46% of the employers replied that their employees were less willing to give up free time than they were five years ago.
   a. 14 employees from these firms are selected at random. Create a probability distribution for the variable counting the number of employees less willing to give up free time than they were five years ago.
   b. What is the probability exactly 10 will be less willing to give up free time?
   c. Use the Cumulative density function and calculate the probability that 10 or less employees in the sample of 14 would be more willing to give up free time.
   d. Calculate the probability that at least 7 employees would be more willing to give up free time.

e. Calculate the probability that between 5 and 9 employees (including 5 and 9) would be more willing to give up their spare time.

3. The Wyatt Company recently conducted a survey on the changing benefits packages offered by midsize and large companies. It was found that 45 percent of the companies offered family leave to care for a sick spouse. If 17 mid to large size companies are selected at random, find the probability that:
   a. Exactly 10 will offer this type of leave.
   b. At least 10 will offer this type of leave.
   c. Less than six will offer this type of leave.

4. In this problem, you'll investigate how the shape of a binomial distribution changes as the value of p changes. Since you'll use n = 10 in each distribution, set the data 0, 1, 2, ...10 in a column named 'x' and use this as the Input column. For parts a to e, construct a binomial probability distribution and store as specified.
   a. Use n = 10 and p = .10 (Store in 'p=.10'.)
   b. Use n = 10 and p = .30 (Store in 'p=.30'.)
   c. Use n = 10 and p = .50 (Store in 'p=.50'.)
   d. Use n = 10 and p = .70 (Store in 'p=.70'.)
   e. Use n = 10 and p = .90 (Store in 'p=.90'.)
   f. Construct Scatter Plots for the outcomes in parts a to e. For each plot use 'x' for the X variable and the stored column values for the Y variable. Connect the points on each of your plots. Compare the results of the plots in parts a through e. Discuss any pattern you might find. How are the distributions skewed? Which distribution is the most symmetric?

5. In this problem you'll investigate the shape of a binomial histogram when the value of n increases while p remains constant. For each part a, b and c, construct an input column with values 0, 1, 2...n. Store the probability values as indicated.
   a. Use p = .25 and n = 10. Store in 'n=10'.
   b. Use p = .25 and n = 50. Store in 'n=50'.

c. Use p = .25 and n = 100 Store in 'n=100'
d. Construct a scatter plot for each distribution and connect the points. Compare the shapes of the plots. Discuss what appears to happen as the value of n increases.

6. A company reports that their computer is "down" an average of 1.2 times during an eight-our shift. In April there will be 630 of these shifts. Set up a simulation that determines the number of times the computer is "down" for each of these shifts.
   a. Use the Tally command to summarize your results.
   b. Create a Session window histogram describing the results.
   c. Use MINITAB to calculate the mean number of "down" times in your simulation. How does this compare to the given mean? If there is a difference in values, explain why.
   d. Use MINITAB to calculate the standard deviation for your simulation data.

7. Getrich Bank records show that an average of 20 people arrive a teller's counter each hour. Use the Poisson distribution to determine the probability that during a one-hour period. Exactly 30 will arrive.
   a. Ten or fewer will arrive.
   b. More than 10 will arrive.

8. Knee flexion, a measure of the knee range of motion is a normally distributed variable. *Physical therapy* reported that the mean knee flexion measure was 132 degrees and the standard deviation 10 degrees.
   a. Simulate the knee flexion measure for a random sample of 600.
   b. Construct a histogram describing your simulation.
   c. Use the Describe command and calculate the mean and the standard deviation for your sample values. How do they compare to the given parameters?

9. Using the parameters given in problem 8, calculate the probability that a person selected at random will have a knee flexion measure of:
   a. Between 125 and 140 degrees
   b. Between 145 and 155 degrees.
   c. More than 160 degrees.
   d. Less than 110 degrees.

10. The Kawasaki Zephyr is reported to have a mean fuel capacity of 4.5 gallons and a standard deviation of .3 gallons.
    a. Simulate the fuel capacity measure of 200 randomly selected Kawasaki Zephyrs.
    b. Construct a histogram for your simulation sample.
    c. Use the Describe command to find the mean and the standard deviation of your sample measures. How do they compare with the given parameters.

11. Find the z-score such that:
    a. 30% of the curve lies to the left of z.
    b. 10 percent of the curve lies to the right of z.
    c. 90 percent of the curve lies between -z and +z.
    d. 20 percent of the curve lies to the right of z.
    e. 5 percent of the curve lies to the left of z.
    f. 95 percent of the curve lies between -z and z.

12. The scores of an entrance exam are normally distributed with a mean and standard deviation of 550 and 95 respectively. Find the entrance score that separates the top 5 percent from the lower 95 percent of the candidates.

13. IQ scores on a particular test are normally distributed with a mean and standard deviation of 100 and 15 respectively, find the IQ above which the top 5% of the population falls.

6. Sampling Concepts

In your statistics class you are discussing the critical role of Central Limit Theorem in inferential statistics. You'll now use MINITAB to simulate experiments that will help you explore the significance of this theorem.

When you've completed this chapter, you should be able to:

- Explain the concepts of the Central Limit Theorem.
- Determine probabilities in sampling distributions.

To begin our illustration of a sampling distribution, you'll play a game. In this game, you will roll a die twice and then calculate the mean of the numbers appearing on top. Of course in rolling a die, you are actually obtaining a random sample from the population of integers 1, 2, 3, 4, 5 and 6. So, when you roll a die twice, you are obtaining a *sample of size two* from the same population. Let the games begin!

THE POPULATION

We'll first examine the properties of the distribution of the population we will be sampling from. Start by forming a column C1 'Pop' consisting of the six values in the population. (Either use the **Set Patterned data** command or type the values into the Data window column along with the name.)

Next construct a Session window histogram of 'Pop' and describe its shape. To do so use the Character graphs in the Windows version or de-select the Hi-Resolution option in the Macintosh and DOS versions.

Note that the histogram produced will be in the form a rectangle. This should not be surprising since each of the six outcomes occurs with an equal frequency. Recall that such a distribution is often called a **Uniform** distribution.

```
Histogram of Pop    N = 6

Midpoint    Count
       1        1  *
       2        1  *
       3        1  *
       4        1  *
       5        1  *
       6        1  *
```

Use the **Describe** command to help you obtain the population mean and population standard deviation. (The output in this command includes *sample* standard deviation = s, so you must use the formula on the right to compute the *population* standard deviation = σ:)

$$\sigma = s\sqrt{\frac{N-1}{N}}$$

```
MTB > Describe  'pop'.

N       MEAN     MEDIAN     TRMEAN      STDEV     SEMEAN
6      3.500      3.500      3.500      1.871      0.764

MIN         MAX          Q1          Q3
1.000      6.000       1.750       5.250
```

and (using the given formula) $\sigma = 1.871\ (.9129) = 1.708$

CREATING THE SAMPLES

Each time you play you will obtain a sample of 2 values. Since you'll play this game 200 times, you'll have 200 samples (n = 2). But let MINITAB do the rolling.

For the first roll of the die choose **Random data** and then **Sample from columns**. **Sample** 200 rows from 'Pop' and **Store** the samples in 'Roll1'. Be sure to select the **Sample with replacement** option. Repeat the process for the second roll but **Store** the samples in 'Roll2'. To compute the mean for each time you play, have MINITAB compute the mean of each row from the **Calc** menu as follows

MACINTOSH	DOS	WINDOWS
Functions and Statistics then **Row Statistics** then Mean	**Functions and Statistics** then **Row Statistics** then Mean.	**Row Statistics** then Mean.

Select **Input variables** 'Roll1' and Roll2' and **Store** the result in 'Means'. Go to the Data window and look at your first few rows to verify that the value in the 'Means' column is simply the sum of the two rolls divided by 2.

THE DISTRIBUTION OF THE SAMPLE MEANS

We will be interested in the distribution of the 'Means' column, so first construct a **histogram** for it. What is its shape? Use the **Describe** command for the values in 'Means'. How does the mean of 'Means' compare to the mean of 'Pop'? Compare the standard deviation of 'Means' with that of the population standard deviation of 'Pop'. Compare the Q_1 and Q_3 values in 'Means' with those in 'Pop'.

```
MTB > Describe 'Means'.

N         MEAN    MEDIAN    TRMEAN     STDEV    SEMEAN
500     3.5990    3.5000    3.6056    1.2787    0.0572

MIN         MAX         Q1         Q3
1.0000    6.0000    2.5000    4.5000
```

Your values will differ since they are the result of a random sampling process. Note that the mean of the 'Means' column is close to the mean of the population but the standard deviation of 'Means' is smaller than that of 'Pop'.

Notes____

____

THE DISTRIBUTION OF THE SAMPLE MEANS

To extend this idea further, let's assume that the game is played an infinite number of times. As you know from your probability studies, the following list represents the 36 possible ways of rolling a die twice . We also know-each way has an equal probability of occurring.

	Die1	Die2		Die1	Die2		Die1	Die2
1	1	1	13	3	1	25	5	1
2	1	2	14	3	2	26	5	2
3	1	3	15	3	3	27	5	3
4	1	4	16	3	4	28	5	4
5	1	5	17	3	5	29	5	5
6	1	6	18	3	6	30	5	6
7	2	1	19	4	1	31	6	1
8	2	2	20	4	2	32	6	2
9	2	3	21	4	3	33	6	3
10	2	4	22	4	4	34	6	4
11	2	5	23	4	5	35	6	5
12	2	6	24	4	6	36	6	6

A quick way to obtain this list is to use the **Set Patterned data** command for each of the two columns. For the first die, **Store the result** in 'Die1'. **Start at 1** and **End at** 6 using an **increment** of 1. **Repeat each value** 6 times, **repeat the whole list** 1 time. For the **second, Store the result** in 'Die2' **Start** at 1 and **End** at 6 and **Repeat each value** 1 time and R**epeat the whole list 6** times.

Now calculate the mean of the two values in each row (select **input variables** 'Die1' and 'Die2') and **Store** the result in the column 'Allmeans'. Go to your Data window and verify that the 36 entries in this new column are:

1.0	1.5	2.0	2.5	3.0	3.5	1.5	2.0	2.5	3.0	3.5	4.0	2.0	2.5
3.0	3.5	4.0	4.5	2.5	3.0	3.5	4.0	4.5	5.0	3.0	3.5	4.0	4.5
5.0	5.5	3.5	4.0	4.5	5.0	5.5	6.0						

★ **Example:** Create a histogram for 'Allmeans' and calculate the mean and the *population* standard deviation for this column. Compare the shape of the histogram and the values of the mean and standard deviation to the corresponding histogram, mean and standard deviation calculated for the population values found in C1.

★ **Solution:**

First create a **histogram** and examine the shape.

```
Histogram of allmeans    N = 36

Midpoint    Count
     1.0        1   *
     1.5        2   **
     2.0        3   ***
     2.5        4   ****
     3.0        5   *****
     3.5        6   ******
     4.0        5   *****
     4.5        4   ****
     5.0        3   ***
     5.5        2   **
     6.0        1   *
```

The shape of the histogram representing all possible sample means (n =2) is symmetric and mound shaped. The histogram for C1 'Pop' was rectangular (representing a uniform distribution.)

Calculate the **mean** and the **standard deviation** of 'Allmeans' using population formulas (since the 36 outcomes represent the entire population).

N	MEAN	MEDIAN	TRMEAN	STDEV	SEMEAN
36	3.500	3.500	3.500	1.225	0.204

MIN	MAX	Q1	Q3
1.000	6.000	2.500	4.500

$$1.225\sqrt{\frac{35}{36}} = 1.208$$

The mean of 'Allmeans' is 3.5 which is the same as the mean of the population in C1. The standard deviation of this distribution of sample means is 1.208. Recall that the standard deviation for the population in C1 is 1.708. Use your calculator to verify the relationship on the right.

$$1.208 = \frac{1.708}{\sqrt{2}}$$

CREATING SAMPLES WITH N = 32

Playing this game so many times has made you an expert, so let's increase the level of difficulty, but first, open a new worksheet. We'll also play this new game 200 times but each time we play we will roll the die 32 times and obtain the mean of the 32 values that land on top.

To make it easier, we'll choose **Random Data** from the Calc menu and choose the **Integer** distribution option. **Generate** 200 rows and **Store** in columns C1-C32. The **minimum** value is 1 and the **maximum** is 6.

Note that each row will represent a sample (n=32) and there will be 200 rows (200 samples). Using the Row statistics command, calculate the **mean** for each sample using **Input variables** from C1-C32. **Store** the result in 'Meanof32'. Go to your Data window and scroll to 'Meanof32'. Each entry in this column represents the mean of 32 values. This is the column of interest to use in our quest to understand the Central Limit Theorem.

★ **Example:** Create a histogram and compute the mean and the standard deviation for the distribution of sample means with n = 32. Compare these results to those for the population values in C1and for those in 'Allmeans'..

★ **Solution:** As before, construct a **histogram** and describe its shape. Use the **Describe** command for 'Meanof32'. Since sampling is involved, results will vary but the histogram will be symmetric and mound shaped.

```
  N        MEAN      MEDIAN     TRMEAN      STDEV     SEMEAN
 200      3.4732     3.4687     3.4711     0.2982     0.0211

   MIN         MAX         Q1         Q3
  2.5937     4.4062     3.2500     3.6562
```

Notice the mean of this distribution of sample means is close to the population mean of 3.5. However, the standard deviation for this sampling distribution is smaller, meaning the sample mean values are less spread out. Verify with your calculator that the standard deviation for your sampling distribution is approximately 1.708 divided by the square root of 32. Compare the values found for the min, max Q_1 and Q_3 to the corresponding ones in the population and in the sampling distribution for n = 2.

notes ____

DETERMINING PROBABILITIES IN A SAMPLING DISTRIBUTION.

In inferential statistics we are often interested in the probability of obtaining a sample mean within a specified interval of values. The results of the Central Limit Theorem are crucial to answering such questions. Let's now look to see how we can use Minitab to answer the probability questions presented in your text.

★ **Examples:** The fuel capacity for all Kawasaki Zephers is normally distributed with a mean of 4.5 gallons and a standard deviation of .7 gallons.

a) If one Kawasaki Zepher is chosen at random from the production line, find the probability it has a fuel capacity of more than 4.7 gallons.

b) A quality control officer tests a sample of 36 Kawasaki Zephers picked at random. What is the probability the mean fuel capacity is more than 4.7 gallons?

c) A quality control officer tests a sample of 100 Kawasaki Zephers picked at random. What is the probability the mean fuel capacity is more than 4.7 gallons?

★ **Solutions:**

a) Since the population is normally distributed, choose **Probability distribution** and then **Normal** distribution from the Calc menu . Select the **Cumulative probability** option. Type 4.5 for the mean and .7 for the **standard deviation.** Use 4.7 for the **Input constant.**

```
MTB > CDF 4.7;
SUBC>    Normal 4.5 .7.
     4.7000     0.6125
```

Examine the Session window output. The first line tells you that you have used the CDF function with an input constant of 4.7. Recall that the result of this command will be P (x ≤ 4.7). The semicolon indicates there is a subcommand. The subcommand specifies a normal distribution with parameters of 4.5 and .7. The output of 0.6125 is then the probability of obtaining a value less than or equal to 4.7. To determine the probability x is *greater* than 4.7, subtract the result from 1. Although you may prefer to use your calculator to perform this operation, we've used Minitab to do so. Our Session window looks like:

```
MTB > Let K1 = 1 - .6125
MTB > Print K1

K1          0.387500
```

We've used the LET command to perform the subtraction and store the result in the constant K1. To display the result, we've used the PRINT command.

There is a .3875 probability (38.75%) of selecting one Zepher from the population and getting over 4.7 miles per gallon with it.

b) Since we're dealing with the mean of a *sample with n ≥ 30*, we apply the Central Limit Theorem and use the Normal distribution probability values. From the Central Limit Theorem we also know the mean of the distribution of means is 4.5 (the same as the mean of the population) but the standard deviation of the distribution of sample means is .1167 (calculated on shown at the left), so use 4.5 in the **mean** text box and but type .1167 in the **standard deviation** text box of the dialog box. The **Input constant** remains 4.7.

$$\sigma_{\bar{x}} = \frac{.7}{\sqrt{36}} = \frac{.7}{6} = .1167$$

```
MTB > CDF 4.7;
SUBC>    Normal 4.5 .1167.
    4.7000     0.9567
MTB > Let K2 = 1-.9567
MTB > Print K2

K2          0.0433000
```

Use the Edit Last Command Dialog option since all you have to change from the previous computation is the standard deviation.

There is a .0433 probability (4.33%) that in a sample of 36 Zephers, the mean of the sample will be more than 4.7 miles per gallon.

c) Return to the dialog box and change the standard deviation to .07 .

$$\sigma_{\bar{x}} = \frac{.7}{\sqrt{100}} = \frac{.7}{10} = .07$$

```
MTB > CDF 4.7;
SUBC>    Normal 4.5 .07.
    4.7000     0.9979
MTB > Let K3 = 1- .9979
MTB > Print K3

K3          0.00209999
```

There is only a .0021 (.21%) chance the mean of a sample of 100 Zephers will be more than 4.7.

Exercises

Create an outfile Chapter6.LIS to record your Session window output.

1. Imagine there are 10 cards placed in a hat. Each card contains a digit (0, 1, 2...9). First, examine this population by entering the values into C1, 'Digits'.
   a. Create a histogram of the population. What is its shape?
   b. Now compute the population mean and population standard deviation.

   To compute the population standard deviation, use $\sigma = s\sqrt{\frac{N-1}{N}} = .9487$

   μ = ________________ σ = ________________

2. Now you'll play a game. Draw a card from the hat at random, write down the number and replace it. Repeat this until you have a sample of 5 digits. You'll then compute the mean of your five digits. Suppose game is repeated 100 times. Use MINITAB to simulate this game. (i.e.draw the values and compute the sample means.) Then you'll examine the distribution of sample means.
   a. Choose Random data and choose Integer distribution from the **Calc** menu. Generate 100 rows and Store in C2-C6. Specify the minimum of 0 and the maximum of 9. Each row will contain a single sample of 5.
   b. Choose Row statistics fromin the **Calc** menu and calculate the mean of each of the 100 samples. Use C2-C6 for Input variables and Store in 'meanof5' .
   c. Create a histogram for 'meanof5' and describe its shape.
   d. Use the Describe command to obtain the statistics for the sample means column 'meanof5'.

   (The N=100 reported by MINITAB is a count on the number of rows of data. We will be interested in n=size of sample, so for this section n=5.)

3. Repeat the exercise forming rows of 100 samples, with each sample having 20 members. Use C9-C28 for the members of these new samples.
   a. Use Row Statistics to compute the mean of each of these samples. Put the results in 'meanof20' (C29).
   b. Graph a histogram for C29 to display the distribution of sample means.

4. Repeat the exercise again forming 100 rows of samples, each sample having 40 members. Use C30-C69.
   a. Use row statistics to compute the mean of each of these samples. Place the results in 'meanof40'. (C70)
   b. Graph a histogram for C70.

5. Now compare the *population* distribution with the distributions of the *sample means* for sample sizes of n=5, n=20 and n=40.

Use the Describe command in the Stat menu. Select C1 'digits' to describe the original population, C7 'meanof5', C29 'meanof20 and C70 'meanof=40' for the distributions of sample means.

Fill in the following table with the simulated results from MINITAB.

	Population	'meanof5'	'meanof20'	'meanof40'
a. Histogram shape				
b. mean				
c. st. dev.	σ=	s=	s=	s=
d. minimum				
e. maximum				
f. Q_1				
g. Q_3				

6. Now review the theory from your text and fill in: According to the Central Limit Theorem: If samples of size n with $n \geq 30$ are drawn from any population

which has a mean = μ and a standard deviation = σ, regardless of the shape of the distribution of the population, or if samples of *any size* are drawn from a population which is *normally distributed* then the distribution of the sample means $\bar{x}$ will have a distribution with: A shape that is approximately ___________. A mean equal to ____________. A standard deviation equal to ______________.

7. The results in the preceding chart were obtained from a simulation. Fill in the following chart with values obtained by using the Central Limit formulas found in your text.

	Population dist.	$\bar{x}$ dist n=5	$\bar{x}$ dist n=20	$\bar{x}$ dist n=40
a. Mean				
b. St.Dev.	σ=	$\sigma_{\bar{x}}$=	$\sigma_{\bar{x}}$=	$\sigma_{\bar{x}}$=

Write a brief essay describing how this exercise illustrates the Central Limit Theorem. Compare and contrast the experimental results you obtained with the theoretical results. What happens to the mean and to the standard deviation of this distribution (of $\bar{x}$) as you increase the sample size?

Use MINITAB to answer the following questions.

8. The breaking strength of a material is normally distributed with a population mean of 85 pounds and a standard deviation of 18 pounds. What is the probability that the mean breaking strength for a sample of 12 pieces of this material will have a breaking strength less than 90 pounds?

9. *U.S. News and World Report*, March 23, 1992 reports that the average Graduate Management Aptitude Test (GMAT) test scores for all students entering the graduate school of business at The University of Texas at Austin was 631 with a standard deviation of 80. Find the probability that the mean of a random sample of 40 students there will be between 600 and 650.

7. Estimating Parameters

In this chapter, you will investigate the meaning of a confidence interval as you simulate the construction of many such intervals from a given population. In addition, you'll learn about MINITAB'S powerful macro facility so that you can create and store programs on your own. Finally you'll learn to use MINITAB to construct confidence intervals.

When you've completed this chapter you should be able to.

- Graphically display confidence intervals.
- Store a macro.
- Run (execute) a macro.
- Edit a macro.
- Form confidence intervals for μ when σ is known or the sample is large.
- Form confidence intervals for μ when σ is unknown.
- Use a macro to form confidence intervals for π.

As you learned in class, confidence intervals are used to estimate an unknown population parameter with a given level of certainty. In an actual situation, the value of the population mean is unknown, otherwise you would not need to estimate it. However, to illustrate the concepts underlying a confidence interval, you will construct 40 such confidence intervals for the mean of a familiar population so, in this case the value of μ will be already known. In the following simulation, you'll use the ten digits 0 to 9 as your population. (It's easy to verify that $\mu = 4.5$.)

INTRODUCING THE MACRO

In addition, while performing this simulated experiment, you will see how you can use MINITAB to produce a stored set of commands called a *macro.*

Macros come in handy for performing tasks that are not preprogrammed into MINITAB since once you have saved commands in a macro, you can run it as many times as you wish.

So far most of the MINITAB commands you have issued have been through the pull down menus. You've also seen how Minitab keeps a Session window record of all the commands as they are executed. By this time you are familiar with such commands as Let, Describe and Print that can also be typed directly after the MTB > prompt in the Session window. In fact, almost all of MINITAB's commands can be issued by from the Session window. (In the Macintosh and Windows version the executed commands are also recorded in a separate window called the History window.) Before we begin to store our commands in a macro, let's first simulate the construction of 40 confidence intervals for the mean of the population of integers 0 to 9.

SIMULATING THE CONFIDENCE INTERVALS

To construct the 40 confidence intervals, begin by generating 40 random samples from the population of the 10 digits. Choose **Random Data** and then **Integer** from the Calc menu. **Generate** 40 rows of data and **Store** them in columns C1-C35. The **minimum** and **maximum** values are 0 and 9.

The random data are displayed in the Data window. Go to the Session window to compare what you typed in the dialog box to the contents of the Session window.

```
MTB > Random 40 c1-c35;
SUBC>   Integer 0 9.
```

The MINITAB command to generate random data is called "Random" and the "C1-C35" tells MINITAB to store the results in columns 1 to 35. The semicolon at the end of the command indicates that a subcommand follows this command. To make it easy to identify commands and subcommands, the subcommand is automatically indented in the Session window. The subcommand "Integer 0 9" tells MINITAB which distribution to sample from.(In this case the Integer distribution from 0 to 9.) The period at the end of the subcommand indicates that no other subcommands will follow.

Now you are ready to calculate the mean of each sample. Choose **Row statistics** as follows:

MACINTOSH	DOS	WINDOWS
Functions and Statistics then **Row Statistics** in the Stat menu.	**Functions and Statistics** then **Row Statistics** in the Stat menu.	From the Calc menu.

Now select the **Mean** option. Use columns C1- C35 for **Input variables** and **Store** the results in 'xbar'(C36). Return to the **Row statistics** dialog box, and calculate the standard deviation of each sample and **Store** the results in 'stdev' (C37). Your Session window will add:

```
MTB > Name c36 = 'xbar'
MTB > RMean c1-c35 'xbar'.
MTB > Name c37 = 'stdev'
MTB > RStDev c1-c35 'stdev'.
```

You will now have MINITAB calculate the error of estimate for each of your 40 samples. From this you will optain the corresponding lower and upper bounds for each sample.

Type each of the following commands after the MTB> prompt in the Session window (screen). Hit ↵ **Enter** after each line.

```
Name C61 'Error'
Name C70 'Lbound'
Name C71 'Ubound'
Let C61 =1.645*'stdev'/Sqrt(35)
Let C70 = 'xbar'- C61
Let C71 = 'xbar'+ C61
Print C36 -C37 C61 C70-C71
```

> When entering commands from the Session window, it's important to include the single quote marks around each column name.

You'll now see 5 columns printed in the Session window. The last two represent the lower and upper bounds for each of the confidence intervals.

CREATING A GRAPHIC DISPLAY OF THE INTERVALS

Create a column with the numbers 1 to 40. You'll use this column to number your samples on the horizontal axis. To do so, use the **Set Patterned Data** command. Put the data into 'Number', **Start** at 1 ans **End** at 40.

In order to construct a horizontal line at the mean, create a column with the the value 4.5 entered into 40 rows. To do so, return to the **Set Pattered data** dialog box and **Store** the results in column 'mu'. Select the **Arbitrary List of Constants** button and type 4.5. **Repeat each value** 40 times.

Now you're ready to construct the graphic display. You will construct three graphs (one for the upper bound, one for the lower bound and the third for the mean) on the same coordinate system. Go to the **Graph** menu and follow the instructions for the platform you are using. Label your graph to produce an attractive display with the **Annotate** option. Use a title of 90% Confidence Intervals and type your name in the footnote space.

MACINTOSH	DOS	WINDOWS
Choose **Multiple Scatter** Plot. Select 'Ubound' the first vertical axis 'Lbound' for the second vertical axis and 'Mu' for the third vertical axis. Select 'Number' for the horizontal axis for all three plots. Choose the **Lines** option and select 'Mu' for Y and 'Number' for X. Choose **Print Window** from the File menu	Choose **Multiple Scatter Plot.** Select 'Ubound' the first vertical axis 'Lbound' for the second vertical axis and 'Mu' for the third vertical axis. Select 'Number' for the horizontal axis for all three plots. Choose the **Lines** option and select 'Mu' for Y and 'Number' for X. Type **P** to print the graph.	Choose **Plot.** Select 'Mu', 'Ubound' and 'LBound' for Y values in the first 3 rows and select 'Number' for each of the three X values. To obtain a line at 4.5, Select **Annotation** then select **Line**. Type 1 4.5 40 4.5 in the points text box to list the coordinates for the two end points of the line. Click on **Frame** and choose **Multiple graphs.** Click to **overlay graphs on the same page.**

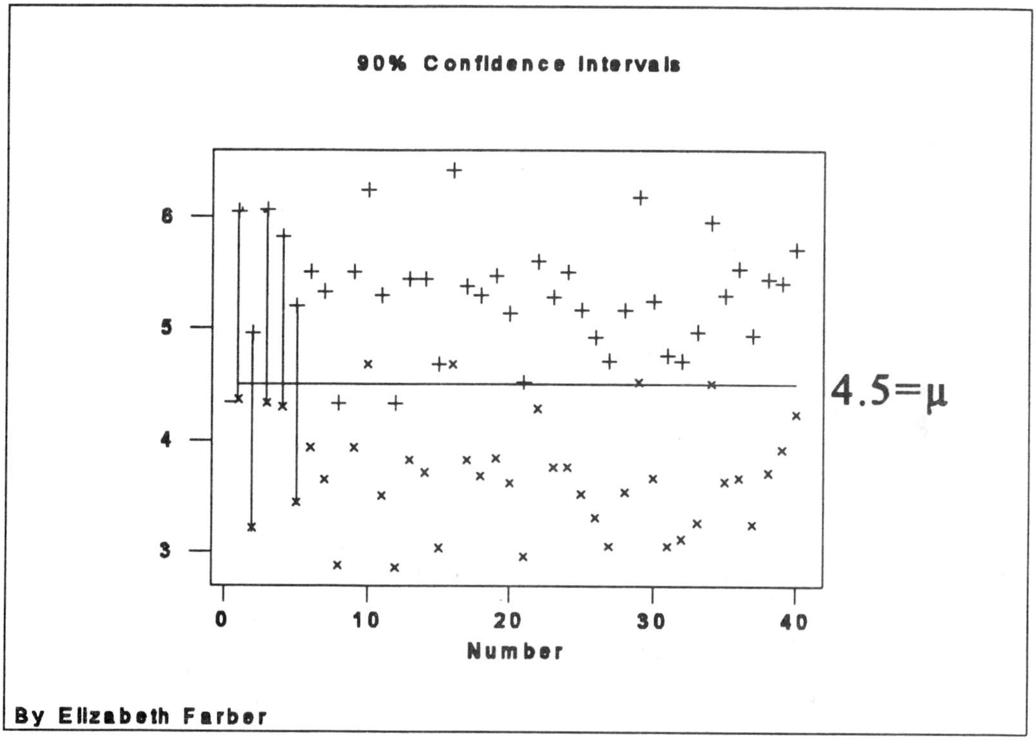

Your graph symbols may be different (on the Macintosh and DOS versions the symbols A, B and C are used), but you'll produce a graph similar to the one above. On your graph printout, use a ruler and draw a vertical line connecting each upper bound symbol to its corresponding lower bound symbol. To illustrate, we've drawn the first five intervals on the above printout. Do you have any vertical lines that do not span across your horizontal line at 4.5?

End your outfile (choose Stop Recording Session from the File menu) and print it. On the printout, place an * next to each interval which does *not* include 4.5. (This will happen if either the lower bound is more than 4.5 or the upper bound is less than 4.5). Now you can place a corresponding asterisk on your graph on any interval that does not span 4.5.

Calculate the percent of intervals which do span the population mean of 4.5. The percent of intervals that span 4.5 is _______________.

RETURNING TO THE MACRO

Let's now extend this idea by generating a total of 200 samples and see how many of the 200 confidence intervals fail to trap the mean. You could of course repeat the previous steps 4 more times, but it is simpler to store the already used commands in a macro and then execute the macro.

To store commands in a macro, Choose **File then Other Files** then **Start Storing Macro** (in Windows **Start Recording Exec**). Select the drive with your data disk and type 90%CI in the filename text box.

Note that the prompt in the Session window has changed from MTB> to STOR>, indicating that MINITAB is storing commands for a macro. When MINITAB is in this mode it will not execute any commands issued, but simply store them. (The commands will be stored in a text file which can be retrieved into a word processing program.)

You now have several options. You could type the macro commands in the Session window. But it is far easier to copy and paste the commands that have already worked. This method has the advantage of letting you try the commands in a given sequence beforehand, verifying that the macro will perform as you intend. Also, since you are copying and pasting commands that have worked correctly, there will be no typing errors.

In the Session window scroll back up to the line `MTB > Random 40 c1-c35;` Place the I-beam to the left of this command and drag it down and to the right until you get to the Print command. Release the mouse. Choose **Copy** from the [Edit] menu.(In the Macintosh and Windows versions you may also go to the History window and copy the commands found there. In the Dos version

Exercises

The data for the exercises in this chapter are found in '7Data.MTW'. Create an outfile for your Session window results. Anaylze the output for each of the given problems and complete the answers in sentence form.

1. *The American Journal of Psychiatry* published the results of a study to determine whether there was a possible type of brain dysfunction associated with infantile autism. Each child in the study was given a behavioral test and scored on a scale from 0 to 116 where 0 = absence of symptoms and 116= maximum severity. The scores of the 21 children in the study were:

   27 35 65 67 47 46 63 44 34 51 17 40 41 60 24 48 29 73 60 41 27

   (Assume the scores on this test are normally distributed.)

   a. Form a 90% confidence interval for μ.
   b. Form a 95%confidence interval for μ.
   c. Form a 99% confidence interval for μ.
   d. Compare the answers for parts a-c. What happens to the width of the interval as the level of confidence increases.

2. To study the characteristics of first-episode schizophrenic patients sample data was collected for 32 patients. The number of years of education for the sample members is listed in '7Exer.MTW' in C3 'YearsEd'.
   a. Construct a 95% confidence interval for the mean number of years of education for all such patients.
   b. Construct a 98% confidence interval for the mean number of years of education.
   c. Compare your answers for parts a and b.

3. Each year, *Money* consultants compile a list of 50 top blue chip stocks, analyze them and suggest which ones to buy, which ones to hold and which ones to sell. The following is a random sample of 9 of the stock prices on this list.

31.25 33.50 104.75 25.50 53.25 57.25 30.75 35.00 58.50

a. Enter the data into MINITAB and construct a 90% confidence interval for the population mean.

b. Suppose another 9 stocks were added to the list. The prices for the second group of nine stocks were exactly the same as the given prices for the first sample of 9. Enter the 18 values (the given 9 values copied twice) forming a new column. Form a 90% confidence interval for the population mean.

c. Compare the results from parts a and b. What seems to happen as you increase the sample size? Test this hypothesis by forming a column with 36 values-(each of the given values listed 4 times).

4. A recent issue of *The Lancet* published an article describing a study of 12 patients concerning the effects of increased inspired oxygen concentrations on exercise performance in chronic heart failure. The oxygen consumption measures during the exercise test (ml/min per kg) were:

9.7 21.0 14.3 15.2 12.8 8.6 10.9 8.3 19.1 7.0 19.5 12.5

a. Construct a 95% confidence interval for the population mean.

5. An IQ test was administered to a sample of 26 chronic schizophrenic patients. For this test, the population values are known to be normally distributed. The sample scores are in c4 'IQ'.

a. Construct a 90% confidence interval for the mean IQ of the population of chronic schizophrenic patients.

b. Assume the population standard deviation is 15. Construct a 90% confidence interval for the mean IQ of these patients.

c. Compare your answers from part a and b. How does a known population standard deviation affect a confidence interval?

6. To determine expenditures in caring for patients with demential who live at home as published in *The American Journal of Public Health*. 141 caregivers returned surveys. Data from these surveys is in '7Exer.MTW' in C5 'Caregive'.

Form a confidence interval at the 90 percent level for the population average number of caregiver hours.

7. Frieda Paine, a physical therapist, is testing a new technique on patients who are recovering from sports injuries. To estimate the average length of time she spent with each of these patients last week, she randomly selects a sample of 10. The data are in C6 'Prob7'
   a. Construct a 95% confidence interval for the week's mean time spent with the population of patients in the testing of the new technique.
   b. Form a 95 percent confidence interval for the population standard deviation for Ms. Paine's patients.

8. 864 requests for MRI (Magnetic Resonance Imaging) scans were evaluated. In 502 cases, the physician had an ownership interest in the facility.(*The New England Journal of Medicine)*
   a. Use the PINTERVAL macro to form a 90% confidence interval for the population percent.
   b. Use the PINTERVAL macro to form a 95% confidence interval for the population percent.
   c. Use the PINTERVAL macro to form a 99% confidence interval for the population percent. .
   d. Compare the results of parts a, b and c for this question. What happens to the confidence interval as you increase the level of confidence?

9. *The American Journal of Psychiatry* reported the findings of a study of HIV-Related risk behaviors among adolescents. Of the 76 psychiatrically hospitalized adolescents in the sample, 40 reported they were sexually active. Use the PINTERVAL macro to form a 95% confidence interval for the percent of psychiatrically hospitalized adolescents that are sexually active.

10. An article in *Focus on Critical Care AACN* reported on a fellowship program in Washington Hospital Center, Washington D.C. to train graduate nurses to work in intensive care units (ICU's). Of the 46 nurses who began the ICU

Fellowship program, twenty-seven are currently working in the ICU's. Use the PINTERVAL macro to form a 95 percent confidence interval for the percent of nurses who begin the ICU Fellowship program and currently work in the ICU.

Going Beyond

The macro you wrote to form the 90% confidence intervals was recorded as a text file. To see it (and print it out if you want) open any word processing program and retrieve '90%CI.MTB' (if necessary, change drives).

You can now edit any part of this program. So, on the first line type: Note This is a Confidence Interval Macro by Yourname. (Anything you type after the word Note will appear on the screen but will not affect the program.)
You can also annotate your program by typing a # (Shift key and 3) followed by any comments you wish to make. At the MTB > prompt type:

Generate 40 random samples which each have 35 members.

This comment will not appear on your screen but will serve as documentation for anyone who reads the program. Insert any additional annotation comments and save the file.

You can use the macro you have already written to write a macro that will generate 50 samples with 40 members each and form confidence intervals at the 95% level. As long as you have saved the original macro, you can now type over it, make any changes you wish and save the new macro with a new name. Use Note and # to annotate it. Save this new macro as **text** only and name it '95%CI'. Return to MINITAB and execute the new macro 5 times so that you again have 200 confidence intervals. Print your results and identify the intervals which do not span 4.5. Count the proportion which span the population mean of 4.5.

8. Testing Hypotheses:
One Sample Procedures

In this chapter you'll simulate a hypothesis testing situation that will help you better understand the concepts of hypothesis testing. You will also learn how to use MINITAB to test hypotheses about a population parameter using one-sample procedures.

When you have completed this chapter you should be able to:

- Test a hypothesis about μ with a large sample (known σ.)
- Test a hypothesis about μ using a small sample.
- Test a hypothesis about a population proportion.
- Test a hypothesis about a population variance.

SIMULATION EXERCISE

In the following exercise you will repeat a one-sample hypothesis test about a population mean 250 times. You'll follow the procedures outlined in your text and eventually make a decision to accept or reject H_0 for each of your 250 samples. Since you will actually *know* the value of the population mean, you'll be able to evaluate your statistical decision to see whether it is correct or whether you have made a type I error (decided to reject the H_0 when it is, in fact true). Finally, you'll determine the proportion of times you have committed a Type I error.

For the population of values, we'll use the integers 1 to 99. Use the **Set Patterned data** command to store this sequence into C1 'Pop'. You'll need to compute the mean and standard deviation of the *population.* Start with the **Describe** command and determine the mean of 'Pop' is 50 and standard deviation using the *sample* formula is 28.72. Since

$$\sigma = 28.72\sqrt{\frac{98}{99}} = 28.5746$$

it will be necessary to use the population standard deviation, we can then compute it as 28.5746. using the formula shown.

For this simulation you'll use a left tail test with a .05 level of significance.

So the null and the alternate hypotheses are: H_0: $\mu = 50$ and H_1: $\mu < 50$ with $\alpha = .05$.

To perform the test, you will draw 200 samples of n = 32 from the given population. This is a simple task for MINITAB! Choose **Random Data** then **Integer** distribution from the Calc menu. **Generate** 200 rows and **Store** the samples in C2-C33. The minimum and maximum values are 1 and 99.

```
MTB > Random 200 c2-c33;
SUBC>   Integer 1 99.
```

Once the samples are drawn, compute the mean for each. Use the **Row mean** command and **Store** the result in 'xbar' (C34).

```
MTB > Name c34 = 'xbar'
MTB > RMean c2-c33 'xbar'.
```

Since the samples are over 30 the sampling distribution for this test is Normal and since $\alpha = .05$. the critical z-score is z =-1.645. Use the decision rule for this test : Reject the H_0 if the corresponding z score is less than - 1.645, otherwise accept it.

Now make the necessary computations and convert each of the sample means into a z-score. From the Calc menu, select...

If you are using the Student Edition of Minitab you may be running out of room, so delete the columns that contain the original data values. To do so just type Erase c2-c33 after the MTB > prompt.

MACINTOSH	DOS	WINDOWS
Functions and Statistics then General Expressions	**Functions and Statistics then General Expressions**	**Mathematical Expressions**

Name the new column 'zscore' and carefully type ('xbar' -50)/(28.5746/sqrt(32)) in the **Expression** text box.

```
MTB > Name c35 = 'zscore'
MTB > Let 'zscore' =('xbar'-50)/(28.5746/sqrt(32))
```

Now that the z-scores for each sample mean have been computed, it will be easier to make the 200 decisions if the column containing the z scores is sorted. **Sort** C2-C35 and **Sort by** the column 'zscore'. **Store the sorted columns** back into C2-C35. When the sort is complete, go to the **Data** window and use the decision rule to make the statistical decision to accept or reject the null hypothesis for each of the 200 rows. (If you erased c2-c33, simply sort c34-c35.)

```
MTB > Sort c2-c35 c2-c35;
SUBC>    By 'zscore'.
```

Recall that we know that the null hypothesis is actually true. Count the number of rows for which you rejected it and thereby making a type I error. What proportion of the rows did you make a Type I error of rejecting a true null hypothesis? On what proportion of rows was your decision to accept H_0 a correct one? Would you be happy with the percent of correct solutions on an ordinary test?

*Notes*____

____

P-VALUES IN HYPOTHESIS TESTS

In the exercise you just completed, you used a traditional method for the hypothesis test. Let's take a look at the p-value method since it is the one easiest to use with MINITAB. To compute the p-value for each of the 200 samples you generated, choose **Probability Distributions** and then **Normal**. Use the mean and standard deviation for the sampling distribution and enter 50 for the mean and 5.0518 (computed from $28.5746/\sqrt{32}$) for the standard deviation. Then choose **Cumulative probability** and select 'xbar' as the **Input column**. Name the **Optional storage** column 'pvalue'.

```
MTB > Name c36 = 'pvalue'
MTB > CDF 'xbar' 'pvalue';
SUBC>   Normal 50 5.0518.
```

For a left tail test, (such as the one in the simulation) the p-value corresponds to the cumulative probability output. (Naturally for a right tail test, the p-value is the cumulative probability subtracted from 1 and in a two tail test, the p-value is twice the value of the left hand test value.) Since $\alpha = .05$, reject H_0 when the p-value is less than .05. In how many rows did this occur? Compare the decisions with those made using the traditional method. If this test were to be performed at the .01 level, how many times would you have made a Type I error?

*notes*____

____

TESTING A HYPOTHESIS ABOUT THE MEAN USING A LARGE SAMPLE (OR A KNOWN POPULATION STANDARD DEVIATION)

★**Example:** A Tegner activity scale is used to evaluate functional levels pre-and postoperatively to quantify the effect of knee surgery on patient's activity level. (The scale ranges from 0 to 10 where 10 = a professional athlete and 0 = total incapacity.) The preoperative mean on the Tegner scale was 2.2. Two years after experimental ligament replacement surgery a sample of 84 patients were evaluated on the Tegner activity scale. The results of the evaluations are found on '8data.MTW' in C1 'Tegner'. Test the hypothesis that there is significant improvement in knee function two years after surgery. (Test the hypothesis that the Tegner score is greater than 2.2) Use the .01 level of significance.

★**Solution:** The hypotheses are: H_0: $\mu = 2.2$ and H_1: $\mu > 2.2$ with $\alpha =$ .01.Since The sample size is greater than 30, you can assume that the population standard deviation is equal to that of the sample and perform a z-test (test with known standard deviation). First use the **Describe** command to obtain the sample mean and standard deviation.

```
MTB > Describe  'Tegner'.
N       MEAN    MEDIAN    TRMEAN     STDEV    SEMEAN
84      4.905    5.000     4.908     1.973     0.215
```

Choose **Basic Statistics** and then choose **1-sample Z** from the **Stat** menu. Select 'Tegner" as the variable. Choose the **Test mean** option, type 2.2 in the text box and choose the greater than **alternative hypothesis** using the pull down menu. Type the ("known") value of **Sigma** 1.973 obtained from the Describe command.

```
MTB > ZTest 2.2 2.236 'Tegner';
SUBC>   Alternative 1.

TEST OF MU = 2.200 VS MU G.T. 2.200
The assumed sigma = 1.97

N       MEAN     STDEV    SE MEAN        Z    P VALUE
84      4.905    1.973      0.215    12.56     0.0000
```

Using the classical method of hypothesis testing you will reject the null hypothesis if the z test statistic is greater than 2.33. MINITAB reports the test ratio to be a z-score of 12.56 and since this is certainly greater than 2.33, it falls in the critical region. Reject the null hypothesis and accept the alternative that conclude the mean is greater than 2.2 and there has been a significant improvement.

Using the p-value approach is simpler. The p-value is reported to be 0 which is less than the level of significance of .01. Reject the H_0 and conclude that there is a significant improvement two years after the experimental surgery.

TESTING A HYPOTHESIS ABOUT THE MEAN USING A SMALL SAMPLE

★**Example:** According to *Career Development Quarterly*, men had a mean response of 15.08 on their evaluation of the importance of opportunity for advancement (in a Life Roles Inventory questionnaire.) The responses for the same question for a sample of 27 women are found in C2 'Liferole'. Test the hypothesis that women rate advancement lower in importance than do men in career decision making. Use the .01 level of significance. (Assume the responses are normally distributed.)

★**Solution:** H_0: $\mu = 15.08$ and H_1: $\mu < 15.08$ with $\alpha = .01$. Choose **Basic Statistics** and then **1-Sample T** from the Stat menu. Click on the **Test mean** option and type 15.08 in the text box. Select the less than Alternative hypothesis.

```
MTB > TTest 15.08 'Liferole';
SUBC>   Alternative -1.

TEST OF MU = 15.080 VS MU L.T. 15.080

N      MEAN     STDEV    SE MEAN        T      P VALUE
27   14.481     2.082     0.401     -1.49       0.074
```

MINITAB reports a t value of -1.49 which corresponds to a p-value of .074. Using the p-value method of hypothesis testing we'll conclude that since .074 is greater than the level of significance, accept H_0 that for this question, women's responses are the same as those of men.

TESTING A HYPOTHESIS ABOUT A PERCENTAGE

MINITAB does not have a command to test a hypothesis about a population percentage. On your data disk you will find a macro 'Ptest' written for Minitab Inc. that can be used to do the job.

★**Example:** A study of 1,710 high school students found that 150 had suffered from an anxiety order at one time in their lives. Test the hypothesis that more than 6 percent of high school student suffer from some type of anxiety disorder. Use the .01 level of significance.

★**Solution** : H_0: $\pi = 6$ percent (.06) and H_1: $\pi \neq 6$ percent with $\alpha = .01$. To use the macro, choose Other Files then Execute macro (Run an Exec in Windows). Select 'Ptest' from your data disk.

```
Execute 'C:\MTBWIN\MANUAL\PTEST.MTB' 1.
Executing from file: C:\MTBWIN\MANUAL\PTEST.MTB
```

Enter the values at the "DATA>" prompt

1. Pi the hypothesized value of the population proportion; (enter as a decimal)
2. x, the observed number of successes; and
3. n, the total sample size.

```
DATA> .06 150 1710
```

You will then by instructed to let Minitab know the type of test you are performing so you will see:

```
At the "DATA>" prompt below, enter a
     1 to perform an right-tailed test, or
     0 to perform a two-tailed test, or
    -1 to perform a left-tailed test.
```

Since you are doing a right tailed test, type 1 at the prompt.

Minitab will print the hypotheses, the z test statistic and it's p-value.

```
Ho: p = 0.0600   vs.   Ha: p   >   0.0600

z = 4.05199        p-value = 0.00003
```

Using the classical method of testing you will reject the null hypothesis if the z statistic is greater than 2.33. Since z = 4.05199 is greater than 2.33, reject H_o. If you prefer the p-value approach, then reject H_o since the p-value of .00003 is less than the level of significance of .01. With either method you will conclude that more than 6% of high school students suffer from some type of anxiety disorder.

HYPOTHESIS TEST FOR A POPULATION VARIANCE:

It's easy to conduct a χ^2 test for the population variance (and standard deviation) using MINITAB. Let's look at an example.

★**Example:** A new machine distributes 8 oz. soft drinks. The contents of a sample of 16 cups were measured and the results entered in C3 'Drinks'. Test the hypothesis that the variance is less than .5. Use the .01 level of significance.

★ **Solution:** The hypotheses are: H_0: $\sigma^2 = .5$ and H_1: $\sigma^2 < .5$ with $\alpha = .01$.Use a calculator to determine the χ^2 test statistic. (Or use the Let and Print commands in MINITAB). $\chi^2 = 15(.35)/.5 = 10.5$. To find the critical value, choose **Probability Distributions** then choose **Chisquare.** Select the **Inverse Cumulative probability**

$$\chi^2 = \frac{(n-1)s^2}{\sigma^2}$$

option. Enter 15 for the **degrees of freedom** and .05 for the **Input constant**.

```
MTB > InvCDF .05;
SUBC>   Chisquare 15.
    0.0500    7.2609
MTB >
```

MINITAB reports that the critical value for the test is 7.2609. The null hypothesis will be rejected if χ^2 is less than 7.2609. Since the χ^2 test ratio of 10.5 is not in the critical region, accept the H_0 that the population variance is .5.

You might prefer to use the p-value approach for this test. In doing so you will calculate the probability that χ^2 is less than 10.5 in a χ^2 distribution with 15 degrees of freedom. Choose **Probability Distributions** then choose **Chisquare.** Select the **Cumulative probability** option. Enter 15 for the **degrees of freedom** and 10.5 for the **Input constant**.

```
MTB > CDF 10.5;
SUBC>   Chisquare 15.
   10.5000    0.2128
MTB >
```

The probability that χ^2 is less than 10.5 is .2128. Since this value is greater than .05 (the level of significance) accept the null hypothesis that the population variance is less than .5.

*notes*____

Exercises

The data necessary to perform the hypothesis tests for the following problems can be found on your data disk in '8Exercise.MTW'. The data has been entered into the column corresponding to the problem number (data for problem 1 will be in C1 etc.).

1. Responses to a survey of sales marketing executives to a question of how often they experienced tension at their jobs are found in C1 'Tension'. (Responses were on a Likert scale of 1 to 5 where 1 represented "never" and 5 "always".) Test the hypothesis at the .01 level that the mean response for sales marketing executives on the question of tension from their job is equal to 2. *The Journal of Marketing*

2. According to *Management Accounting* the average salary for Certified Management Accountants (CMA's) who are in the field less than one year is $31,129. The average first year salary for a sample of 15 CMA's is given in C2 'CMAsal'. Test the hypothesis that the average for first year CMA's is different than $31,129. Use the .05 level of significance.

3. Cellular Phones are becoming more and more popular. *Consumer Reports*, Jan 1993 reported the following prices for a sample of cellular phones.

   $499 $279 $669 $550 $207 $600 $399 $100$235$467
   $249 $200 $235 $489 $300 $299 $200$200$249

   a. Enter the values into C6 'Phones' and test the hypothesis at the .05 level that the average cost for a cellular phone is more than $300.
   b. Test the hypothesis that the standard deviation is more than $150. Use the .05 level.

4. A Research and Development survey for the San Francisco Council on the Homeless found at the time of the study there was a bed capacity of 1,395 available for homeless people in San Francisco. 54 of these beds were available for shelters serving battered women and their children. Test the

hypothesis that shelters for battered women and their children have less than 5 percent of the total beds available in that city. Use the .05 level of significance.

5. Over a long period of time it has been determined that the average purchase for shoppers in a large book store is $14.35. To determine the effect of touching on customer behavior, 15 shoppers were approached by three male and 3 female experimenters as they entered this store and handed a catalog. During alternate one-hour periods, the experimenter either touched the subject lightly on the upper arm or did not. The purchase prices for the shoppers who were touched are found in C5 'Touch'.
   a. Test the hypothesis at the .05 level of significance that shoppers who are touched will spend more than $14.35
   b. Test the hypothesis that the standard deviation for the purchase price is more than $2.00.

6. In 1987 48 percent of nursing home residents had behavioral problems. A recent study of 6629 nursing home residents found that 1392 had behavioral problems. Test the hypothesis at the .01 level that less than 48 percent of 1990 nursing home residents have behavioral problems. *National Medical Expenditures Survey.*

7. The mean score on a 10 item test (0-3 points each) of Calculus concepts for all students enrolled in a traditional Calculus course at Duke University was 9.64. Project CALC course is radically different from the traditional course since it emphasizes interactive computer laboratories, cooperative learning and extensive student writing. To evaluate the success of Project CALC, a test was given to students enrolled in a Project CALC section. The scores are found in C7 'CALC'. Test the hypothesis that the mean score for the Project CALC students is higher than 9.64. Use the .05 level of significance. (*The Project CALC Newsletter*)

8. 1,192 students in kindergarten and first grade in Southern Arizona took the Language Assessment Scales (LAS) test to determine a students's dominant language. It was found that English was the dominant language for 357 of them. Test the hypothesis that 30 percent of students in kindergarten and first grade in Southern Arizona English as their dominant language. Use $\alpha = .05$. *The Journal of Educational Issues of Language*

9. The Department of Commerce estimates a 4 percent failure rate for franchisors. Economists believe that this rate is higher. In a study of 55 franchises, three volunteered that they had failed. Test the economists' claim. Use the .01 level of significance. *The Journal of Small Business Management*

10. *The Journal of Small Business Management* reported on research conducted to assess the behavior of retail apparel buyers. Buyers from independently owned clothing stores were asked to indicate the importance of factors that influence their purchasing decisions. (The rating was on a 5-point Likert scale from 1= not at all important to 5= extremely important.) The responses of 309 buyers who were asked to rate the importance of trade publications as an information source is found in C10 'Buyers'. Test the hypothesis at the .05 level that the mean rating is greater than 3.

11. A sample of 24 college students were asked how much time they spent watching television on a weekday. Data is in C1 'Boobtube'
    a. Test the hypothesis that the mean time college students watch television is more than 120 minutes. Use the .01 level of significance.
    b. Test the hypothesis that the variance for the time college students spend watching television each week night is more than 10,000. Use the .01 level of significance.

12. It is estimated that 60 percent of assaults involve drugs and/or alcohol. The Journal of Research in Crime and Delinquency reported out of 69 assaults, 43 involved drugs and/or alcohol. Test the hypothesis at the .01 level that the

rate of assault crimes that involve drugs and/or alcohol is 60 percent. *The Journal of Research in Crime and Delinquency*

13. A study was done to assess the effect of Captopril on patients with congestive heart failure. The data is in C13 'Captoprl'. Test the hypothesis at the .01 level that the variance for patients who take Captopril is less than 4. *The American Heart Journal* Aug.

14. 1985A tire manufacturer claims the average life of its deluxe radial tires is 75,000 miles. A random sample of 21 of these tires is road tested and the data is found in C14 'Tires'. Would you accept the manufacturers claim at the .05 level?

15. *USA Today* (July 6, 1993) reported the results of a survey to determine television is a reflection of real life. Among the 94 shows surveyed, 48 depicted at least one act of violence. Test the hypothesis that the percent of shows on television that depict violence is higher than 50 percent. Use the .01 level of significance.

16. Patients with medical back problems requested MRI scans. The cost for the patients in the sample is found in C16 'MRI'. Test the hypothesis that the average cost for an MRI patients with back problems is equal to $1000. Use the .01 level of significance. *The New England Journal of Medicine*

17. A study of juvenile delinquent boys was published in Criminal Justice and Behavior. The IQ scores for a sample of delinquent boys is found in C17 'IQ'. Test the hypothesis that the mean IQ for juvenile delinquent boys is lower than 100. Use the .05 level of significance.

18. The U.S. Federal Highway Administration Selected Highway statistics and Charts annual reports that in 1989 there were a total a 9,898 thousand passenger cars sold. Of these 7,073 thousand were domestic models. Test the

hypothesis that over 70 percent of the passenger cars sold in 1989 were domestic. Use the .01 level of significance.

19. The change of intention scale is a self-reported measure on a scale of -9 to 9. The change of intention score of a sample of customers for name brand items after learning of a 20% discount in the price of the items is given in C19 'CofI'. Test the hypothesis that at the given discount level the population mean change of intention value is 4.5. Use the .05 level of significance. *Journal of Consumer Research*

20. Transcutaneous electrical nerve stimulation (TENS) devises are frequently used in management of acute and chronic pain conditions. An important component of the TENS system is the skin electrode. A study in Physical Therapy (Oct. 1991) was done to determine conductive differences among electrodes used with TENS devises. For the first trial of the 11 electrodes in the low-impedance group the impedance measures (in ohms) were:
    1200 1200 1000 1600 1400 1400 1200 1700 1600 1300 1600
    Test the hypothesis that the variance for the impedance measure for the first trial of the low impedance electrodes is less than 100. Use the .05 level of significance. *Journal of Physical Therapy*

21. The perceived discount PD is measured by PD = (perceived regular price - perceived sale price)/perceived regular price. At Nordstrom's the actual discount was 20%. The PD for a sample of customers is given in C21 'PD'. Test the hypothesis that the mean PD rating at Nordstrom's was less than the actual discount of 20 percent. Use $\alpha = .05$. *Journal of Consumer Research*

22. A Tegner activity scale is used to evaluate functional levels pre-and postoperatively to quantify the effect of knee surgery on patient's activity level. The scale ranges from 0 to 10 where 10 = a professional athlete and 0 = total incapacity. The average Tegner level before injury was 7.0. The Tegner scores for a sample of patients five years after this experimental surgery is given in C22 'Tegner5'. Test the hypothesis that five years after surgery the

Tegner level is back to where it was before injury (i.e. that the Tegner level equals 7) Use α = .05.

23. The standard deviation for the waiting time for 15 customers at the First National Bank and Trust was 1.7 minutes. Test the hypothesis that the population variance is more than 1.5 minutes. Use the .01 level of significance.

24. *USA Today* (July 6, 1993) published the results of a survey to determine how well the characters on T.V. reflect real life. In the U.S. population, 7 percent of all females are redheads. In a sample of 1263 females on television, 139 had red hair. Test the hypothesis at the .05 level that the percent of females who are redheads is higher on television than in real life. (The same survey found 1 television female with blue hair-but that was Bart Simpson's mother, Marge)

25. Normal subjects have a mean score of 76 on the Boston Naming Test score. The results of a study of the effect of Lorazepam on brain glucose metabolism for a sample of 10 alcoholic subjects are found in C25 'BostonNT'. Test the hypothesis that the scores on this test for alcoholic subjects is less than 76. Use the .05 level of significance. *American Journal of Psychology*

26. The length of time a sample of 8th grade students sleep each night is found in C26 'Sleep'. Test the hypothesis at the .01 level that 8th graders sleep 8 hours per night.

27. The mean response from teachers to the statement: "The tests I have taken were generally good assessments of my knowledge of an area." was found to be 4.09. The response was on a scale of 1 to 6 where 1= strongly disagree to 6 = strongly disagree. A sample of 84 sophomore education majors that was asked the same question and the results are in C27 'Soph'.Test the hypothesis that the mean response of sophomore education majors is different than 4.09. Use α = .05. *Journal of Educational Research*

28. A study to examine how well marital dissolution was predicted by husbands' and wife's personality scores was published in *The Journal of Personality and Social Psychology.* The mean rating on a scale for "Agreeableness" for husbands in stable marriages was 27.37. Do husbands in unstable marriages differ? The scores for a sample of 64 husbands in unstable marriages are in C28 'Agree'. Test the hypothesis that husbands in unstable marriages have an agreeableness rating different than 27.37. Use $\alpha = .01$.

29. The cost for a sample of patients who experienced an unscheduled crisis is in C29 'Cost'. Test the hypothesis that the average cost for this type of psychiatric service is less than $5,000. Use $\alpha = .05$.

30. *TV Guide* claims men control the zapper in 41% of the homes. In a survey of 163 families in Portland Oregon, 68 said men control the zapper. Test the hypothesis that men control the zappers in 41 percent of homes in Portland. Use the .05 level of significance.

9. Testing Hypotheses:

Two Sample Procedures

In this chapter you'll explore various hypothesis tests that are used in comparing the parameters of two populations.

When you have completed this chapter you should be able to :

- Test the difference of population means with dependent samples.
- Test for equal population variances.
- Test the difference of two population means with independent samples.

Before you start the following exercises, open '9Data.MTW' from your data disk.

TESTING TWO POPULATION MEANS-DEPENDENT SAMPLES

As you learned in your statistics class, you'll use a test of differences for paired *(dependent)* samples when each measure in one sample corresponds with a measure in a second sample.

★ **Example:** An elementary school teacher in a large school district is testing a new method for teaching mathematics. She gathered 40 pairs of twins and randomly selected one twin (B) from each pair to participate in the experimental instruction. The other twin (A) was taught by traditional methods. After a year a test was given to each twin in both groups. The test scores are found in '9Data.MTW' in 'TwinA and 'TwinB'. Test the hypothesis at the .05 level of significance that there is no significant difference in the scores of the two groups.

★ **Solution:** The hypotheses are: H_0: $\mu_d = 0$ and H_1: $\mu_d \neq 0$ with $\alpha = .05$.

First form a new column that represents the *difference* of scores for each pair. You may use the **General Expression** command from the pull down menu or, if you prefer, type the **Let** command into the Session window after the MTW > prompt.

```
MTB > Let 'Diff' = 'TwinB'- 'TwinA'
```

We'll be performing a t-test similar to the ones in Chapter 8 on this column of differences. If the method of teaching makes no difference, then on the average, the *population difference* in scores will be 0. (Note in the Data window that some differences are positive and others negative.)

Choose **Basic statistics** and then **1-Sample t** from the Stat menu. Use 'Diff" for the **variable** and click on the **Test mean** option. Use the default test value of 0 and the **alternative** "not equal"

```
MTB > TTest 0.0 'Diff';
SUBC>   Alternative 0.

TEST OF MU = 0.00 VS MU N.E. 0.00

N       MEAN     STDEV    SE MEAN       T     P VALUE
40      3.42      7.65     1.21       2.83    .0073
```

Note that the t statistic of 2.83 and the corresponding p-value of .0073 are reported. Since .0073 is less than the level of significance of .05, reject the null hypothesis and conclude that the experimental method made a significant difference in the test scores.

TESTING THE DIFFERENCES IN MEANS-INDEPENDENT SAMPLES

For testing the difference in population means using independent samples, we can use a 2-Sample t test regardless of the size of the samples. MINITAB does not provide a separate z- test since for large samples the t-distribution values are very close to those of the standard normal distribution (z).

★ **Example:** After short term hospital stays a sample of 110 disabled elderly subjects were given to an experimental group that offered physician-led primary home care with a 24-hour service. 73 disabled elderly in a control group were offered ordinary care. After 6 months both groups were tested on the MMSE (mini-mental state examination with a range of scores 0-30). The test scores for each group are found in 'MMSEexp' and 'MMSEctrl' in '9Data.MTW'. Use a hypothesis test at the .05 level to test the hypothesis that the experimental group did significantly better.

★ **Solution:** Since the samples are independent, a two sample t test is in order. First we have to determine whether the variances for the two populations are likely to be equal.

The hypotheses are: $H_0 : \sigma_1^2 = \sigma_2^2$ and $H_1 : \sigma_1^2 \neq \sigma_2^2$

Though there is no command that executes a F-test for equal variances, we can use the commands of MINITAB to help us obtain the necessary components of such a test. First compute the sample standard deviation in each column.

```
MTB > StDev 'MMSEexp' k1.
   ST.DEV. =       4.5669
MTB > StDev 'MMSEctrl' k2.
   ST.DEV. =       7.0698
```

Since K2 >K1, use the control group in the numerator of the F ratio. The F ratio can be computed using the Let command as follows:

```
MTB > Let k3 = k2**2/k1**2
MTB > print k3

K3          2.39650
```

The F ratio for the test

Now compute the critical F value. Choose **Probability Distributions** and then **F** from the Calc menu. Select the **Inverse Cumulative probability** option and select 'MMSEctrl' for the first variable and 'MMSEexp' for the second. The numerator has 73-1 =72 degrees of freedom and the denominator has 110-1 = 109. For a two tail test at the .05 level of significance, use the **Input constant** at .975. (.025 is in the right tail.)

```
MTB > InvCDF .975;
SUBC>   F 72 109.
    0.9750     1.5136
```

Since the F ratio of 2.3965 >1.5136, reject the null hypothesis and conclude that thc variances are not equal.

Now you are ready for the t test for unequal variances, so choose **Basic Statistics** and then **2-Sample t**. Use the **alternative** 'greater than' and . level of confidence of .90 since .05 of the curve will be in the right tail.

```
MTB > TwoSample 90 'MMSEctrl' 'MMSEexp';
SUBC>   Alternative 1.

TWOSAMPLE T FOR MMSEctrl VS MMSEexp
             N      MEAN      STDEV   SE MEAN
MMSEctrl    73     24.36       7.07      0.83
MMSEexp    110     23.54       4.57      0.44

90 PCT CI FOR MU MMSEctrl - MU MMSEexp: ( -0.73,  2.37)

TTEST MU MMSEctrl = MU MMSEexp (VS GT): T= 0.88  P=0.19
 DF=  111
```

Notice the mean, the standard deviation and the standard error for each of the groups is included in the output. A 90% confidence interval is computed for the *difference* of the two groups. When this confidence interval includes 0, it is likely that there is *no difference* between the measures in the groups. On the last line, MINITAB describes the command with the option GT (greater than) and reports the t value and the corresponding p value.

The p-value of .19 > .05 so accept the null hypothesis that there is no significant difference between the group's scores on the MMSE.

★ **Example:** In a study of the effect of Lorazepam on brain glucose metabolism there were 13 normal subjects and 10 alcoholic subjects. The verbal IQ for the normal subjects is found in '9Data.MTW' in 'VerbalN' and for the alcoholic sample in 'VerbalA'. Test the hypothesis that the IQ of alcoholics is lower than that of normal people. Use the .05 level of significance.

★ **Solution:** The members of the samples are not paired, so we'll do a 2- sample t test for independent samples. First do an F test to determine whether the population variances are likely to be equal. The hypotheses are: $H_0 : \sigma_1^2 = \sigma_2^2$ and $H_1 : \sigma_1^2 \neq \sigma_2^2$. Begin with computing the standard deviation for each sample and then computing the ratio of the variances.

```
MTB > StDev 'VerbalN' k1.
   ST.DEV. =       20.499

 MTB > StDev 'verbalA' k2.
   ST.DEV. =       13.857

MTB > let k3 = k1**2/k2**2
MTB > print k3
```

K3 2.18837 *The F ratio*

Next find the critical F value. Choose **Probability Distributions** and then **F** from the Calc menu. Select the **Inverse cumulative probability** option. The numerator has 12 degrees of freedom (13-1) and the denominator has 9 (10-1). Since α is .05 and this is a 2 tail test, use .9750 for the **Input constant**.

```
MTB > InvCDF .975;
SUBC>   F 12 9.
    0.9750    3.8682
```

Since the test ratio 2.18837 < The critical F, accept the null hypothesis that the population variances are equal.

Now we can proceed to use the t test for populations with equal variances, so choose **Basic statistics** and then **2-Sample t** from the Stat menu. We'll use the greater than **alternative** and select the **equal variances** option so the pooled standard deviation will be computed.

```
MTB > TwoSample 90 'VerbalN' 'verbalA';
SUBC>   Alternative 1;
SUBC>   Pooled.

TWOSAMPLE T FOR VerbalN VS verbalA
           N      MEAN      STDEV   SE MEAN
VerbalN   13     112.8       20.5       5.7
verbalA   10     111.3       13.9       4.4

90 PCT CI FOR MU VerbalN - MU verbalA: ( -11.5,  14.5)

TTEST MU VerbalN = MU verbalA (VS GT): T= 0.19  P=0.42
DF=  21

POOLED STDEV =       18.0
```

Since the p-value .42 > .05, accept the null hypothesis. There is no significant difference in the verbal IQ of alcoholic and normal groups.

*notes*____

Exercises

The data for these exercises is found on '9Exerc.MTW'. Create an outfile for your Session window output. Include all hypothesis test steps for your answers.

1. The perceived discount PD is measured by PD = (perceived regular price - perceived sale price)/perceived regular price. A study was done to determine if the PD for high-image stores (such as Nordstrom's) is higher than for that of low-image store (such as May's). The PD data are found in C1 NordstPD' and C2 'MayPD'. Test the hypothesis that the PD at Nordstrom's is higher than that for The May Company. Use the .01 level of significance.

2. *Fortune* Magazine listed "America's Most Admired Corporations". Senior executives were asked to rate the ten largest companies in their own industry based on specified attributes. The ratings for the Computers and Office Equipment Industry are found in C3 'CompOff' and those for the electronic industry are found in C4 'Electron'. Test the hypothesis that ratings in the Computer and Office Equipment industry are lower than those in the Electronics industry. Use the .05 level of significance. (Assume both populations are normally distributed.)

3. A trial was conducted to evaluate the effectiveness of a work-site health promotion program in reducing obesity. 16 work-sites were randomly selected to receive treatment of weight control classes combined with payroll incentives. 16 work sites served as controls and received no treatment. Test the hypothesis at the .01 level of significance that there was no difference in BMI for the control group before and after the treatment. Data is found in C6 'BMI' and Subscripts are in C7 'Group'. (1=experimental group and 2 = control group).

4. To research the influence of touch on consumers' evaluation of service, experimenters were trained as servers in a restaurant. In alternating hours the servers either touched or did not touch the diners. The ratings for the groups

are found in C8 Touch' and C9 'NoTouch'. Test the hypothesis at the .05 level that the mean rating for diners who are touched is higher than the mean rating for those who are not.

5. Primary caregivers of patients were interviewed and asked to keep diaries. After 6 months, 141 returned diaries and 123 did not return diaries. The time spent as caregiver for the those returning the diaries and those not returning them are found in C10 'Return' and C11 'NoReturn'. Test the hypothesis at the .01 level that there was no difference in time spent as caregiver between the two groups.

6. Participants in a consumer product research study were randomly divided into two groups, given four types of orange juice to sample and asked to rate the test quality for each. 29 subjects in the first group were given one brand to drink at a time letting about five minutes elapse between consecutive samples during which time subjects were asked to eat a cracker. In the second group, the 29 subjects were given all four brands simultaneously and were instructed to go back and forth between the different brands and were not provided with crackers. The taste quality ratings for the groups are found in C12 'onetime' and C13 'together'. At the .01 level of significance, test the hypothesis that there will be a lower mean taste quality when one brand is tried at a time than when all brands are tried simultaneously.

7. *Macworld,* published results of tests that were performed to compare various software slide maker speeds at high resolution (4k) and medium resolution (2K). The speeds in seconds to produce a simple text with logo image are found in C14 'MedRes' and C15 'HiRes'. Test the hypothesis that the high resolution slides took significantly more time. Use the .05 level of significance.

8. A study involved individual measures of neuropsychological functioning for chronic schizophrenic patients and those of normal subjects. Scores for both groups on the Wide Range Achievement test (WRAT) are found in C16

'Schizoph' and C17 'Normal'. Test the hypothesis at the .01 level that there is no difference in WRAT scores for the two groups. (Assume both populations are normally distributed.)

9. A test was conducted to determine the effectiveness of using an anti-inflammatory cream on delayed-onset muscle soreness. Ten patients were treated with the cream on one arm and with a placebo on the other. After four days a measure of muscle (on a visual-analogue scale) was then taken for each patient on each arm. The patient numbers are found in C18 'Patient' and the results are in C19 'CtrlArm' and C20 'TreatArm'. Test the hypothesis that there is less pain in the treated arm. Use $\alpha = .01$.

10. How well can divorce be predicted by a wife's personality score? Five years after their marriage 222 couples remained together and 64 dissolved their marriages. As newlyweds all wives (and husbands too, but that's another question) were given a personality test and then rated on "dysfunctional beliefs." The ratings of the wives for "dysfunctional beliefs" are found in C22 'Married' and C23 'Divorced'. Test the hypothesis that there is no difference in the wife's dysfunctional beliefs for the two types groups. Use α =.05. *The Journal of Personality and Social Psychology.*

11. An experimental fat diet was followed by 36 people. The cholesterol level for each was measured before and after the diet. Test the hypothesis that there is a significant decrease in cholesterol level after the diet. Use the .01 level of significance. The participants are listed in C23 'Subject' and the data are in C24 'before' and C25 'after'.

12. In a study of the effect of Lorazepam on brain glucose metabolism 5 alcoholic subjects were given Lorazepan and 5 were given a placebo. The metabolic values at the thalamus (μmol/100g/min) for each of the groups are found in C26 'Loraz' and C27 'Placebo'. Test the hypothesis that metabolic rates measured at the thalamus are no different for alcoholics given a placebo

and those given Lorazepam. Use $\alpha = .01$. *American Journal of Psychology*, (Assume both populations are normally distributed)

13. The duration of single limb support (SLS) for a sample of 25 amputees using a type of artificial foot was measured on the prosthetic side and on the intact side. Subject numbers are given in C28 'Amputee' and the SLS duration (in seconds) is given in pairs in C29 'prosth' and C30 'intact'. Test the hypothesis at $\alpha = .05$ that there is no difference in duration of SLS between the artificial side and the intact side. (Assume both populations are normally distributed.)

14. A measure of the right atrial pressure (mm Hg) was made for cardiac patients who were given Captopril and for those given Nitroprusside. The measures (in mm Hg.) are given in C31 'Captoprl' and C32 'Nitropr'. Test the hypothesis that there is no difference in right atrial pressure between the two groups. Use the .01 level of significance. (Assume both measures are normally distributed.)

15. Do men and women have different values when determining a career. The paired responses to a sample of values identified in a Life Roles Inventory published in *Career Development Quarterly* are found in C33 'Male' and C34 'Female. Perform a test of paired differences. Use $\alpha = .01$

16. An article in *Criminal Justice and Behavior* claims that an intellectual imbalance of performance IQ with verbal IQ (P > V) is a useful predictor of the probability of becoming delinquent. Delinquency scores are found in C35 'HighP>V' and C36 'LowP>V'. Test the hypothesis at the .01 level that there is no difference in the delinquency scores for these two groups. Use $\alpha = .05$.

17. What do members of the American Bowling Congress (ABC) do to relax away from the office? The answer is that they bowl. *Bowling Magazine*, published the first team averages for the ABC Office Men's League for this year for the previous year. The data are in C40 'ThisYear' and C41 'LastYear'. Test the hypothesis that there is no difference in scores from last year to this year. Use $\alpha = .05$.

10. Quality Control

In this chapter you'll learn to construct and interpret several types of statistical process control (SPC) charts using MINITAB.

When you have completed this chapter you should be able to:

- Construct and interpret an Individuals chart
- Construct and interpret $\bar{x}$ and R charts.
- Construct and interpret p-Charts.
- Identify other conditions indicating a process is out of control.

Statistical Process Control (SPC) is used all over the world to monitor the quality of goods and services. Control charts - graphical displays comparing the data of a current process to a set of control limits- are an important tool of SPC. With MINITAB you can produce a variety of control charts for quantitative as well as qualitative data. In this chapter we'll look at the Individuals chart, the $\bar{x}$ chart, the R chart and the p chart.

Data for each control chart is entered in columns in time sequence. For each type of chart, MINITAB computes the values for the Center Line (CL), the Upper Control Limit (UCL) and the Lower Control Limit (LCL). Recall that data falling above the UCL or below the LCL indicates that something out of the ordinary is probably taking place taking place in the process. A process is said to be "out of control" when any data falls beyond the control limits.

USING AN INDIVIDUALS CONTROL CHART

Let's first look at how a control chart can be used to plot individual values, since this type of chart is not only the easiest but also the most economical to use. For an individuals chart, we'll have to assume that the data is normally distributed.

★ **Example** : Justin Thyme is the chief quality control officer at Highqual Corporation, a firm that manufactures roller bearings that are used as components in tractors. He has determined from previous batches that the population mean diameter of these bearings is 55 centimeters and the population standard deviation 1 centimeter. The diameters of the first 30 roller bearings that are produced in the 8-4 shift have been measured by assembly line workers.. The data and their observation numbers are recorded in 'Diameter' in '10Data.MTW'. Produce an individuals control chart and determine whether the process is in statistical control.

★ **Solution** Select SPC charts then Individuals (in Windows select Control Charts and then Individuals) from the Stat menu. Select 'Diameter' as the variable.

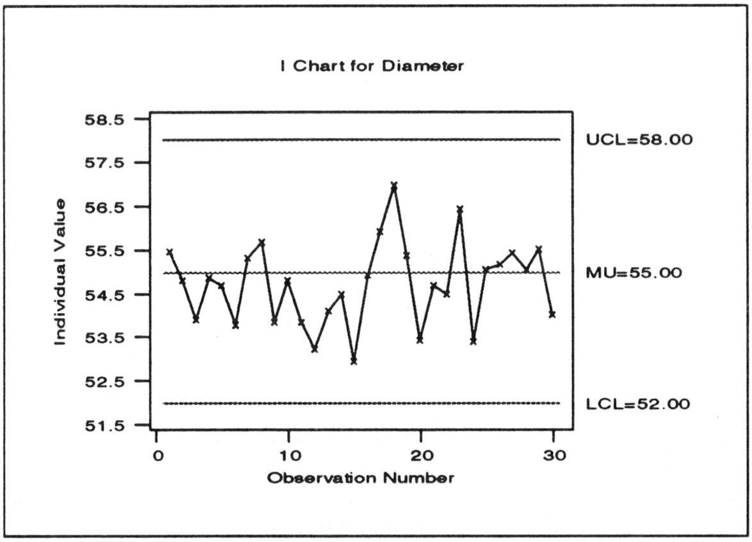

Type 55 in the Historical Mu box and for the standard deviation, click on Historical under the Sigma choices and type 1 in the box. MINITAB will produce a control chart similar to the one shown. Notice that the center line is labeled as Mu =55. The UCL is 58 (3 standard deviations above the mean) and the LCL is 52 (three standard deviations below). Since all data values fall between the control limits, we can say that the process is in control. Any variation in measure is normal and natural.

★ **Example** : Penny Urndt, managing director of the CPA firm Dollars & Senz, is hoping to improve client service. One of the most important customer requests is prompt delivery of financial reports. Determine whether her firm was "in control" in this area by creating a control chart from the data given in 'Delivery'. The data represents the number of working days it took to deliver clients' financial statement. In the past, the mean time for the final delivery of a financial statement was 14 working days and the standard deviation 1.5 working days.

★ **Solution** Choose Control Charts and then Individuals from the **Stat** menu. The Historical Mu is 14 and the Historical Sigma is 1.5.Your control chart should resemble the one shown. The Center Line is at 14 and the Upper and Lower control limits are 18.5 and 9.5. There are several data values that fall beyond the control limits indicating that the process is probably out of statistical control.

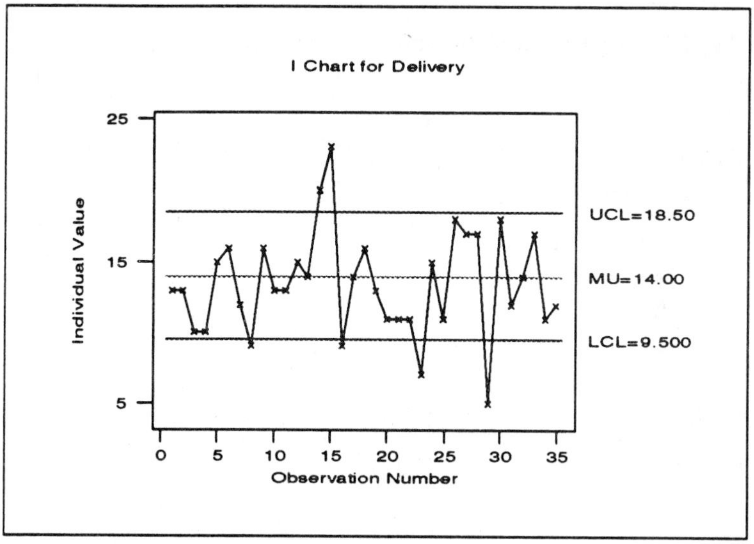

USING $\bar{X}$ AND R CONTROL CHARTS

Since individual values may be subject to a great deal of fluctuation, it is often more desirable to monitor the variability of a process with two charts: one to monitor the mean, and the other to monitor the dispersion. Usually used together, the $\bar{x}$ chart monitors the mean and R chart monitors the variability of a process. To construct these charts, data is gathered in subgroups that have n observations each. Groups of four or five are commonly used in subgroup sample sizes since these sample sizes make data collection easy. In most cases, the population process mean and standard deviation are not known but MINITAB has a way of estimating them. The population process mean can be estimated by the grand mean, $\bar{\bar{x}}$ the mean of the subgroup means.

★ **Example** : A machine is used to automatically fill 12 ounce cans with Zippy Cola. Philip D. Cannes, a production supervisor, takes subgroups of four cans each hour and measures the contents. The results of the first 20 subgroups taken over a 20 hour period are shown found in 'cans'. Construct an $\bar{x}$ and an R chart to see if the process is in statistical control.

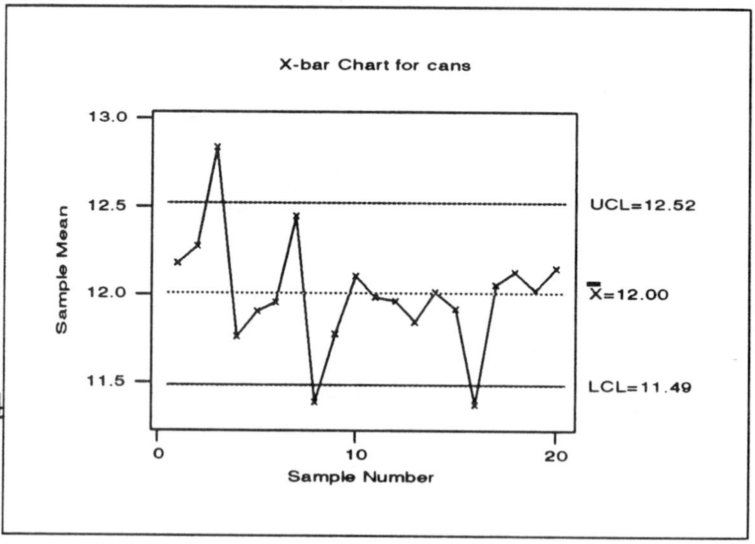

★ **Solution** : For the $\bar{x}$ chart, select Control charts from the Stat menu and select X-bar. Select 'Cans' for the variable and type 4 for the subgroup size. With no historical mean,

MINITAB will use the mean of all the sample means (the grand mean) for the center line. For the control limits, MINITAB will either estimate a pooled standard deviation value, use an Rbar estimate or use a historical value. Select the Rbar estimate method and construct a control chart similar to the one shown. Note that there are three points beyond the control limits so the process is probably out of statistical control.

Next look at the variability of the process in an R chart. Choose R chart from the Control Charts menu. Select 'Cans' for the variable and 4 for the subgroup size. Use the Rbar estimate for the standard deviation. The control chart will be similar to the one shown. The chart indicates the variability of the process is in control.

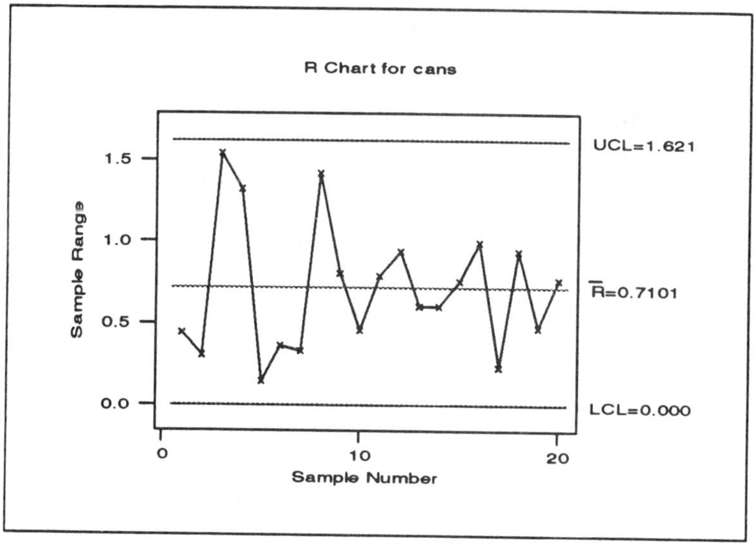

USING P CHARTS

A p-chart measures the proportion of non-conforming (often defective) output in a series. It is used to monitor qualitative data.

★ **Example** : Kara Lott was recently hired to supervise and streamline the welfare system operated by the Department of Social Welfare in New Harmony. Social workers should submit their case reports in 10 days or less from the time clients have been interviewed. Any report submitted after 10 days is classified as "non-conforming". The data in 'Nonconf' represent the number of non-conforming reports Kara has found from a sample of 200 taken each week for 26 weeks. Produce a p-chart to determine if the process of submitting case worker reports is in statistical control.

★ **Solution** :

Choose p chart from the control charts options. Select 'nonconf' for the variable. The subgroup size is 200. When you do not provide a Historical mu, MINITAB will use the mean of the sample proportions for the center line. As with the other control charts, MINITAB will estimate the standard deviation and compute upper and lower control limits. The points in

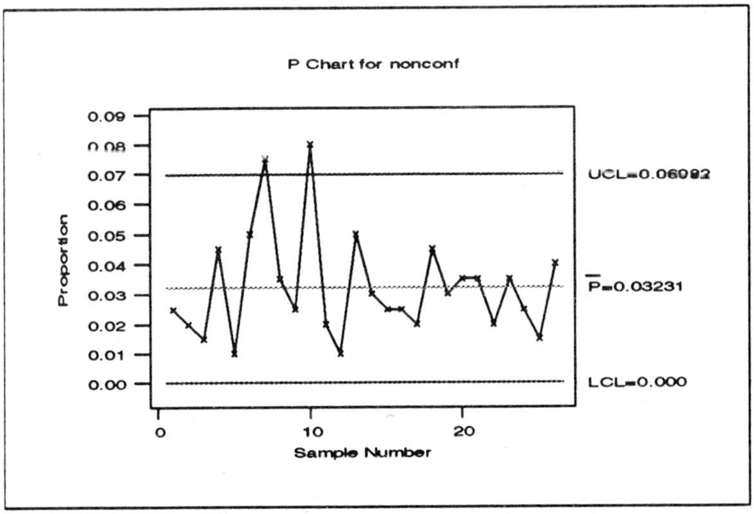

the chart represent the proportion of 'non-conforming' reports in each sample. As you can see from the control chart, there are several weeks where the proportion late case studies is too high. The chart indicates that these occurrences should be looked in to in order to determine the cause.

Other tests for Special Causes

Thus far we have examined control charts and determined a process to be 'out of control' when one or more points falls above the UCL or below the LCL. There are other types of patterns that can be traced by data points that fall between the UCL and the LCL that suggest special types of variation that need to be examined. When the ' special causes' option is selected, MINITAB will alert you to one or all of eight special patterns.

When a point fails a test, MINITAB marks it with the test number on the plot. If a point fails more than one test, MINITAB prints the number of the first test you select in the list and prints a summary table with complete information.

Zone A represents the area up to one standard deviation from the center line
Zone B, the area between one and two standard deviations from the center line,
Zone C, the area between two and three standard deviations from the center line.

1. One point beyond zone A
2. Nine points in a row in zone C or beyond
3. Six points in a row, all increasing or all decreasing
4. Fourteen points in a row, alternating up and down
5. Two out of three points in a row in zone A or beyond
6. Four out of five points in a row in zone B or beyond
7. Fifteen points in a row in zones C, above or below center
8. Eight points in a row beyond zones C, above or below center

★ **Example:** The supervisor at a large factory is looking to do a quality control study of the inventory. If the inventory is too large, the company is loosing money since products are sitting in the plant. If the inventory is too small, orders will not be able to be filled. Over a period of 40 months, she randomly samples 5 days inventory each month. The results are found in 'quality' in '10Data.MTW'. Produce an Xbar control chart and select the option to show special causes.

★ **Solution:** Choose Xbar from the Control chart options. The sample size is 5. Click on the Tests for Special Causes button. All data values fall within the UCL and the LCL, however there are indications that special causes are present. The points marked with the number 2 indicate there are nine points in a row in Zone C or beyond. The number 4 indicates 14 points in a row alternating up and down and the number 6 indicates 4 out of 5 points in Zone B or beyond.

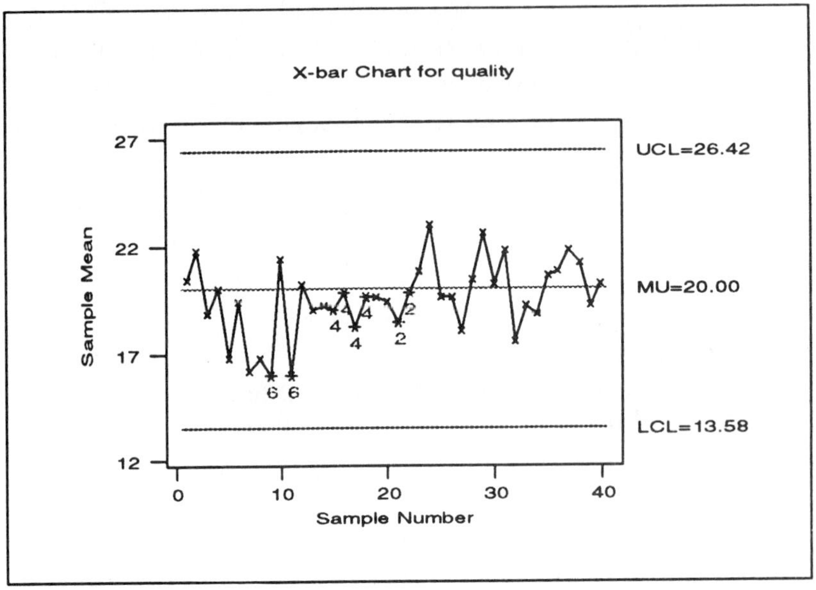

*Notes*____

Exercises

Construct the appropriate control chart for each of the following problems. Select the option for Special Causes. The data for these problems can be found on '10exer.MTW'. Include a written analysis for all problems.

1. At Slurper's Choice bulk shipments of imported coffee beans are freeze dried and made into gourmet instant coffee using a secret recipe. The manager, Ima Brewer, wants to determine if the first stage of the coffee making process is in control so she weights the first 30 packages from an incoming shipment of a new supplier. From past history, she knows the mean weight of each shipment is 45 kg. and the standard deviation 5 kg. Use an individuals control chart to determine whether the process is in statistical control. The data is in 'Weight'.

2. Mort Alitee, the district manager at Sooner or Later Insurance Corp. (SLIC) has observed a decrease in that sales for new policies. He suspects worker morale is low and may be out of control. He has 36 employees respond to a psychological questionnaire from which they will be scored on a morale rating of 1 to 10. In the past, the mean morale rating at the company was 6 and the standard deviation 1.2. Use an individuals control chart to determine whether morale ratings at SLIC are in control. The data for the employees are found in 'Morale'.

3. An essential step in making a certain type of rod is a plating process in which various composite materials are coated with a thin layer of copper. For this process, the temperature of the plating bath must be controlled so that the plating is uniform. The hourly temperatures of the plating bath over a 24 hour period are listed in 'Temp'. In the past the mean temperature has been 110 degrees F and the standard deviation has been .7 degrees F. Use an Individuals control chart to determine whether the process is in statistical control.

4. The Televac company makes thermocouple gauge tubes used to measure pressure in a vacuum. An oxidation process protects a tube during

production. In the past, the average time needed to oxidize a tube was 3.2 seconds and the standard deviation time was .6 seconds. Use an individuals control chart to determine if the data found in 'Time' is in statistical control.

5. The manager at a plant where copper rods are plated has made some personnel changes and wants to see if the temperature of the plating bath is now in control. He takes 4 temperature measures each hour for 24 hours. The data is in 'Temp4'. Use a subgroup size of 4 and an $\bar{x}$ and an R control chart to determine if the process is in statistical control.

6. At the Televac Company the length of the oxidation process is timed and batches of 5 tubes are taken off the production line each hour for 30 hours. Use an $\bar{x}$ and an R control chart to determine if the process is in statistical control. The data is in 'Time5'.

7. A machine used in a production process is supposed to automatically cut aluminum rods into 9 centimeter lengths. At the last inspection, the process was out of control. An industrial engineer has recalibrated some equipment and wants to see if the process is now in control. The data in 'Rods4' represents subgroups of 4 rods sampled each hour for 30 hours.

8. The Escargot Z-968 sports car is painted at a plant in Mobile, Alabama. Each hour during production, 300 cars are painted and thoroughly inspected for bubbles and defects. The data in 'Escarg' gives the number of defective paint jobs found in the samples of 300 taken each hour for a 24 hour period. Use a p-chart to determine if the process is in statistical control.

9. A company produces foam material to be placed inside seat cushions. There are 100 cushion inserts in a batch. Each batch is inspected, and the number of inserts not conforming to specifications is recorded. The data in 'Cushions' represent the number of non-conforming inserts in samples of 35 batches. Use a p-chart to determine if the process is in statistical control.

10. There are 800 teachers employed in a local school district. An administrator keeps records of the number of teachers absent each school day for the first marking period of the year. The data is found in 'absences'. Use a p-chart to determine if the data are in statistical control.

11. A nursing quality assessment program is in place in the intensive care unit(ICU) at Getwell Hospital. The program requires that an admission assessment be completed for each patient within 8 hours. Each day during the month of October a sample of 40 ICU patients is selected. The data in 'assess' represent the number of patients in the daily sample whose admission assessment was not complctcd within 8 hours. Usc a p-chart to test to see if the data are in statistical control.

II. Analysis of Variance

In this chapter you'll explore how to use analysis of variance to test to see if the means of three or more populations are likely to be equal.

When you have completed this chapter you should be able to:

- Perform an Analysis of Variance test for groups in different columns.
- Perform an Analysis of Variance test for groups in the same column.
- Explain the entries in the ANOVA table.

The analysis of variance calculations can be quite tedious- even for tests with very small samples. With MINITAB, however, the ANOVA test is quite easy to perform. MINITAB gives the option of comparing the means of several populations when all sample observations are in one column and all subscripts are in a second. Another option is to compare the means of several populations when the samples from each population are placed in different columns.

TEST WHEN SAMPLES ARE IN DIFFERENT COLUMNS

★ **Example:** It has been estimated that 80% of all lower back pain cases are caused by weak trunk muscles. Studies have suggested that improved strength of the trunk muscles will aid in the prevention and treatment of lower back pain. In a study to compare the effect of various training frequencies on the development of strength participants were randomly assigned to one of four groups. Training group 1 = once every other week. Training group 2 = once a week. Training group 3 = twice a week and Training group 4 = three times a week. The following data represents the weight (kg) for each of the participants at the beginning of the program. Assume all populations are normally distributed and that population variances are equal. Use analysis of variance to test the hypothesis that the mean weights of the four groups are equal. Let α =.05. *Physical Therapy*

group 1	group 2	group 3	group 4
84	56	70	47
93	78	59	73
83	56	78	104
61	61	53	71
121		104	69
67		110	99
		40	

★ **Solution** For this test the hypotheses are:

H_0: The means of all the populations are equal.
H_1: There is at least one group that has a different mean.

Enter the data into four columns. Choose **ANOVA** and then **ONEWAY** (unstacked) from the Stat menu. Select 'group1wt', 'group2wt', 'group3wt' and 'group4wt' for the responses.

The Session window will display an ANOVA table and a table with basic statistics for each group and a 95% confidence interval for the mean of each group. In the confidence interval display, the * represents the sample mean and the ( ) the 95% confidence limits.

```
MTB > AOVOneway 'group1wt'-'group4wt'.

ANALYSIS OF VARIANCE
SOURCE     DF        SS        MS        F        p
FACTOR      3      1220       407     0.87    0.473
ERROR      19      8868       467
TOTAL      22     10088
```

```
                              INDIVIDUAL 95% CI'S FOR MEAN
                                     BASED ON POOLED STDEV
LEVEL      N    MEAN    STDEV ----------+---------+---------+------
group1wt   6   84.83    21.28      (--------*---------)
group2wt   4   62.75    10.44 (----------*-----------)
group3wt   7   73.43    25.97    (--------*-------)
group4wt   6   77.17    21.11     (---------*--------)
                              ----------+---------+---------+------
POOLED STDEV =   21.60                 60        80       100
MTB >
```

In the ANOVA table, the Factor (sometimes called treatment) computations result in an estimate of MS factor or $\sigma^2_{between}$. The Error computations produce an estimate of MS error or σ^2_{within}. The Sum of squares$_{between}$ (Factor) is 1220 and since the degrees of freedom is 4-1=3, the mean square$_{between}$ is 1220/3 =407. The sum of squares$_{within}$ is 8868 so the sum of squares$_{within}$ is 8868/19 = 467. The F ratio is then computed by 407/467 = .87. The p-value is .473 for this test. Since .473 >.05, accept the null hypothesis. The mean weights of all four groups are likely to be the same. The confidence interval graphic confirms the decision. Notice that all confidence intervals overlap.

Now let's look at another example in which the data for all groups is stored in the same column and the subscripts indicating the different factors (treatments) are in another column.

TEST WHEN DATA IS IN ONE COLUMN AND FACTOR IN ANOTHER

★ **Example:** Ms. Anne Tenna, a first year middle school teacher, claims that television viewing habits are the same for students in different middle school grades. She questioned of a sample of her students about how many minutes they watch television each night. The number of hours for each student is in 'TVminute' and the grade level for the corresponding student is in 'grade' of "11data.MTW'. Test Ms. Tenna's claim at the .05 level.

★ **Solution:** First set up your hypotheses:

H_0: The means of all the populations are equal.
H_1: There is at least one group that has a different mean.

The ANOVA table will be as follows:

```
MTB > Oneway 'TVminute' 'Grade'.

ANALYSIS OF VARIANCE ON TVminute
SOURCE      DF        SS        MS        F        p
Grade        2     94969     47485     4.38    0.029
ERROR       17    184098     10829
TOTAL       19    279067


                  INDIVIDUAL 95% CI'S FOR MEAN
                       BASED ON POOLED STDEV
LEVEL  N   MEAN  STDEV   -------+---------+---------+---------
   6   7  274.3  106.3           (-------*--------)
   7   8  114.9   83.2  (------*-------)
   8   5  194.4  130.3      (--------*---------)
                        -------+---------+---------+---------
POOLED STDEV =104.1    100       200       300
MTB >
```

The F ratio for this test is 4.38. The p-value is .029 and since .029 <.05, reject the null hypothesis. There seems to be at least one group that has a different mean. From the confidence interval display, it seems that the seventh graders watch less television than the children in the other grades. (Maybe they're not getting enough homework.)

notes ____

Exercises

The data for these exercises can be found in '11Exerc.MTW'.

1. Four managers were asked to supervise each of four branches of a large bank on a rotating basis. The market share for each branch (in percent of deposits) is given for each manager in C2-C5 'Manager1' 'Manager2' 'Manager3'. Test the hypothesis at the .01 level that there is no difference in the performance of the four managers. *Journal of Retailing*

2. In a test to determine whether mental skills are different for different age groups subjects in their 30's, 50's, 60's and 70's were given a 'digits backward' test. (A psychologist reads a sequence of digits and the subject is asked to recite them in reverse order.) The data represents the number of digits correctly recited for each and is found in C6-C9 'thirties' 'fifties' sixties' and 'seventies'. Test the hypothesis that the means for all four age groups are equal. Use the .01 level of significance.

3. A study in *Physical Therapy* compared the effect of various training frequencies on the development of strength. Training group 1 = once every other week. Training group 2 = once a week. Training group 3 = twice a week and Training group 4 = three times a week. The following data represents the age for each of the participants. Use Analysis of Variance to test the hypothesis that the mean ages for the participants of the four groups are equal. The ages are found in C10-C13 'group1' 'group2' 'group'3 and 'group4'. Use the .05 level of significance.

4. The marketing director for a pasta manufacturer claims that the height of the shelves on which the product is displayed will affect the sales volume. In one store the product was placed at eye level at a second at waist level and at a third store the product was at knee level. The number of products sold for each of eight days were recorded. Is there a significant difference in sales at the .01

level based on the shelf location of the product? The data are found in C14-C16 'eye' 'waist' and 'knee'.

5. A career counselor claims there is no difference in career decision-making attitudes among students from various socio-economic classes. The results of scores from an attitudes test are given in C17-C19 'lower' middle' and 'upper'. Test the counselor's claim at the .01 level. *Career Development Quarterly,*

6. A psychology professor believes that the amount of time his students spend studying is affected by the semester. In a year-long experiment, students were randomly selected during the three different semesters and asked to estimate the number of hours they spent studying per week. The hourly estimates are found in C20-C22 'Summer' 'Fall' and 'Spring'. What should the professor conclude at the .05 level?

7. Due to a clerical error on the part of a chicken farmer, four truckloads of chickens arrive at a processing plant at the same time. The receiving supervisor must select one of the truckloads and send the others back. To determine if the average weights in all four truckloads are the same samples are drawn from each truckload and entered into C23-C26 'Truck1' 'Truck2''Truck3 and 'Truck4'. What decision at the .05 level should the supervisor make?

8. A marketing expert claims that the average market share (in percent) for the top three selling detergents is the same. The data in C27-C29 'Tide' Wisk' and 'Era' represent market share figures taken at various supermarket chains for these detergents. Test the marketing expert's claim at the .05 level. *Journal of Marketing*

9. In a study to measure neuropsychological functioning for first-episode schizophrenic patients, chronic schizophrenic patients and normal comparison subjects each participant was given the Benton Visual Retention Test. The number of error made by individuals in each group is given in C30 'Errors' The

identifying subscripts for the three levels are found in C31 'levels' where level 1 represents first episode schizophrenic patients, level 2 represents chronic schizophrenic patients and level 3 normal patients. Test the hypothesis at the .01 level that the mean number of errors for all three groups is the same. *American Journal of Psychiatry*

10. Researchers at a leading pharmaceutical company want to determine if the three leading brands of aspirin are really different from each other in terms of speed of relief. Volunteers were randomly assigned to use brand A brand B or brand C. Each was instructed to take the recommended dosage when a headache began and to record the number of minutes that elapsed before they got relief. Use the data (in minutes) in C32 Brand and the Subscripts in C33 'abc' to conduct an analysis of variance at $\alpha = .05$. Is there a significant difference in the speed of relief?

11. An industrial engineer wants to determine if the four machines in operation are performing with equal efficiency. Random samples of 100 have been drawn at various times from each of the machines and the number of products in each batch that do not meet specifications are recorded. The data are found in C37-C37 'machinea' ' machineb' ' machinec' and 'machined'

12. Scores on measures of emotional distress are given for nicotine-dependent smokers, nondependent smokers and nonsmokers. Test the hypothesis at the .01 level that there is no difference in the mean scores for the three groups. The data are in C38 'Distress' and the subscripts are in C39 'group'. *American Journal of Psychiatry*

13. The sales manager of Floppydisk Software wants to determine if a dress code will have an effect on sales. In an experiment, sales persons were selected to wear either Business Suits, Casual Outfits or Jeans in visiting prospective clients. The sales (in thousands of dollars) for a 4-week period

have been recorded in C41-C43 'business', 'Casual' and 'Jeans' Use analysis of variance to make a statistical decision at the .05 level about a dress code.

14. Health Care is a significant expense for employers. A benefits technician claims that the per-employee average cost for traditional indemnity (fee for service), for Health Maintenance Organizations (HMOs) and for preferred provider organizations were equal. The data in C44-C46 'indemnity', 'HMO' and 'PPO' was collected by A. Foster Higgins &Co. a benefits consulting firm. Test the claim of the benefits technician at the .01 level. *Nation's Business*

Going Beyond

When you perfprm with an Analysis of Variance test, it is important to check that the assumptions for the test are satisfied otherwise the test may not be valid. The following assumptions are made with each ANVOA test:

1) The populations in the study have normal distributions.

2) Each sample is drawn randomly and each sample is independent of the other samples.

3) The populations from which the sample values are obtained all have the same (unknown) variance.

Perhaps you were wondering about the validity of these assumptions for the tests you have been perfoming. MINITAB can be useful in determining whether or not it is reasonable to make these assumptions.

To check the assumption for normality, **Stack** all samples in the same column and select the **subscript** option. When you open the ANOVA oneway dialog box, select the options to **Store residuals** and **Store Fits.** After you execute the ANOVA command, go to the Data window where you'll see columns containing the residuals and the fitted values. The fitted values in oneway analysis of variance are equal to the means of the corresponding samples and the residuals are the differences between the data value and the fitted value for each row. You can use the residuals to check the normality condition for the pooled samples.

To obtain a Normal probability plot (NPP) that will determine whether it is reasonable to assume the data is from normally distributed populations, first compute a z-score for each residual. From the **Calc** menu, choose **Functions.** When the dialog box opens, select the residual column as the **Input** column. Type zscore for the column name where you'll store the results. Then select **Normal scores** (the last option). MINITAB will compute the zscores and store them. You'll use a scatter plot to plot these zscores against the residuals. If the plot is close to a straight line plot, then it is reasonable to assume the condition of normality is satisfied.

Choose **Scatter Plot (Plot** in Windows) from the **Graph** menu. Then use 'zscore' for the vertical (Y) axis and 'Resi' for the horizontal (X). Examine the plot. If it is close to a straight line, then the test for analysis of variance is valid.

The **boxplot** can be a helpful way of visually checking the assumption that the variances of all the populations are equal. When the data is stacked in one column, produce a boxplot for each factor by using the **by variable** option. Are the boxes approximately the same length? If they ar not there is an indication that the variances are *not* equal. Return to problem 1 and check that the necessary assumptions are met. Continue with each of the given problems and check the assumptions.

12. Chi-Square Tests

In this chapter you'll use several types of chi-square tests to perform statistical tests on qualitative data.

When you have completed this chapter you should be able to:

- Perform a Chi-square test of independence of variables.
- Perform a goodness-of-fit Chi-square test.

When a die is rolled and a coin is tossed, the results are clearly independent. And the results of drawing two cards without replacement from a deck of cards are obviously *not* independent since the pick of the first card will influence the pick of the second. In most cases however it is usually not clear whether or not two variables are independent and so we use a chi-square test to determine whether they are or not.

CHI-SQUARE TEST FOR INDEPENDENCE OF VARIABLES

★ **Example:** After short term hospital stays 110 disabled elderly subjects were given an experimental physician-led primary home care with a 24-hour service. 73 disabled elderly controls were offered ordinary care. The following is a record of the types of complications each group had.

Type of Complication	team patients	control patients	Total
Accidents	25	24	49
Drug side effect	7	6	13
Mistreatment	4	7	11
Total	36	37	73

Test at the .01 level that the percentage of various types of complications was the same for the two groups. *American Journal of Public Health*

★ **Solution:** To test for independence, first enter the observed counts O from each cell into a MINITAB table consisting of numeric columns and rows. In this case use two columns. Note that it is helpful, but not necessary to form an alpha column that describes the row categories and to name each column according to the column category. *Do not enter the totals.*

The hypotheses for this test are:

H_0: The variables are independent and
H_1: The variables are not independent.

$$X^2 = \Sigma \frac{(O-E)^2}{E}$$

Choose **Tables** then **Chisquare Test** from the **Stat** menu. Select the columns 'Team' and 'Control' containing the frequency table. (*You may select up to seven columns and they must contain integer values.*) MINITAB will compute the expected value E for each cell as well as the chi-square statistic.

MINITAB prints a table of observed values and expected values, the total chisquare statistic as the sum of its components from each cell of the table, and the number of degrees of freedom. If there are any cells that have expected values less than five, MINITAB will also list a warning about these.

```
MTB > ChiSquare 'Team' 'Control'.
```

```
Expected counts are printed below observed counts

              Team   Control      Total
     1          25        24         49
             24.16     24.84

     2           7         6         13
              6.41      6.59

     3           4         7         11
              5.42      5.58

Total           36        37         73

ChiSq =  0.029 +  0.028 +
         0.054 +  0.053 +
         0.374 +  0.364 = 0.902
df = 2
```

To find the critical value that separates the acceptance region from the rejection region, you can use the table in your text or use MINITAB. Select **Probability Distributions** from the **Calc** mean and select **Chisquare**. Chose the Inverse Cumulative Probability button and type 2 for the degrees of freedom. This value is reported in the Chisquare printout, but recall that the degrees of freedom = (no. of rows -1) (no. of columns -1). Since the critical region consists of the 1% of the curve that lies farthest to the right, and the Inverse Cumulative density function reports the value that corresponds to the area to the left of the input probability, type .99 as the input constant.

```
MTB > InvCDF .99;
SUBC>   Chisquare 2.
    0.9900     9.2103
MTB >
```

The critical Chi square value is 9.2103. Since the Chi square statistic .902 is not in the critical region, accept the null hypothesis that the type of complication is independent of the type of care provided in this study.

GOODNESS-OF-FIT

★ **Example:** The director of human resources for a large insurance company claims there has been a change from five years ago in the distribution of its management personnel's level of education. His research showed that five years ago the highest level of education for 15 percent of management personnel was a high school diploma, for 64 percent it was a college degree, for 8 percent it was some graduate school and 13 percent had a master's degree or higher. Test the claim at the .05 level that there has been a change. A recent of survey of showed thc following data for 216 currently employed management personnel:

Highest Level of Education	current number
high school diploma	19
college degree	132
graduate school	30
master's degree or higher	35

★ **Solution:** The hypotheses for this test are:

H_0: The distribution for educational level of employees has remained the same as it was 5 years ago.
H_1: There has been a significant change in the distribution of educational level.

Form a column with the observed values and name it 'observed'. Then form a second column 'percent' consisting of the hypothesized probabilities. A column of expected values can then be formed with the Let command. (Use the General Expressions dialog box or type the following directly into the Session window.)

```
MTB > Name c4 = 'expected'
MTB > Let 'expected' = sum ( 'Observed')* 'Percent'/100
```

Use the Let command again to form a column of Chi square entries.

```
MTB > Name c5 = 'chisq'
MTB > Let'chisq' =('Observed'-'expected')**2/'expected'
```

The chi square entries can be computed with:

```
MTB > Name c6 = 'stat'
MTB > Let 'stat' = sum( 'chisq')
MTB > Print 'Level'-'stat'.
```

The entries in your Session window will be:

```
  Level   Observed  Percent  expected  chisq        stat

1 High School  19    15      32.40    5.54198    16.8923
2 College     132    64     138.24    0.28167
3 Graduate Sch 30     8      17.28    9.36333
4 Masters      35    13      28.08    1.70536
```

To find the critical value remember that the chi square curve will have k-1 degrees of freedom where k = the number of categories.

```
MTB > InvCDF .95;
SUBC>   Chisquare 3.
   0.9500     7.8147
MTB >
```

Since the test statistic of `16.8923` falls in the critical region (to the right of `7.8147`) reject the null hypothesis. There is evidence to suggest that the distribution has changed.

Exercises

1. Two different operative techniques were used in clinical trials involving reconstructive knee surgery. Technique A used a hole drilled in the femur and Technique B used an over-the-top reconstruction. The five year results were as follows:

Technique	Failure	Success
A	8	22
B	22	32

Test the hypothesis that the chance of failure is independent of the technique used. $\alpha = .01$. *American Journal of Sports Medicine.*

2. In a study in *The American Journal of Psychiatry* dealt with the characteristics of people who had ever been tobacco smokers. Subjects in a random sample were classified as nicotine-dependent and nondependent. The following data was reported:

Current smoker	Nicotine Dependent Smoker	Nondependent smoker
Yes	169	123
No	33	69

At the .01 level, test if there is a significant difference between the proportion of current smokers (defined as those reporting they had smoked during the year preceding the interview) in the two groups.

3. Participants in a consumer product research study were given four types of orange juice to sample and asked to rate the test quality for each. A random sample of 30 subjects were given one brand to drink at a time letting about five minutes elapse between consecutive samples during which time subjects were asked to eat a cracker. The following shows the indicated preferences:

Brand	Number Preferring
A	10
B	8
C	5
D	7

Use $\alpha = .01$ and test the hypothesis that there was an equal preference for each brand (a uniform distribution).

4. To test the fairness of a die, it is rolled 100 times. A 1 showed up 15 times, a 2 showed 20 times a 3 showed 22 times a 4 showed 13 times, a 5 showed 19 times and a 6 showed up 11 times. Test the hypothesis that the die is fair. Use the .05 level of significance.

5. Are marital status and race independent variables for those who have legal abortions? Use the following data (numbers in thousands) from The Centers for Disease Control to test the independence of the variables at the .01 level.

	White	Black/Other
Married	68	31
Unmarried	279	141

6. A recent study in *The American Journal of Public Health)* to examined specific smoking habits of physicians in Minnesota. Use the following data to

test the independence of age and smoking status at the .05 level of significance.

Age	Current Smokers	Former Smokers	Never Smokers
less than 40	5	33	94
40-49	13	48	62
over 50	17	64	53

7. A politician running for county supervisor is planning his campaign strategy on the issue of gun control and wants to know if there is a significant difference in the percentage of voters who favor the issue between district A, district B and district C. A random sample of 355 voters yields the following data:

District	In favor	Opposed
A	89	46
B	65	45
C	60	50

Test the hypothesis that there is no difference in percentage favoring gun control among the three districts. Use $\alpha = .05$

8. *The New York Times,* Jan 1993 reported that in 1979 the distribution of non-farm employment was 23 percent in the manufacturing sector, 19 percent in the services sector, 6 percent in finance, insurance and real estate, 17 percent in retail, 18 percent in government, 5 percent in construction, and 12 percent other. In 1992, out of 108.4 million workers, the distribution was as follows:

Sector	Number (in millions)
Manufacturing	18.4
Services	29.3
Finance ins. real est.	5.4
Retail	19.5
Government	18.4
Construction	4.3
Other	13.1

Test the hypothesis at the .05 level that the distribution of non-farm workers has changed since 1979. (Source: Bureau of Labor Statistics)

9. The production manager of a company that does steel plating claims that some shifts have a higher percent of defects than others do. The following data were collected during a 24-hour period:

Shift	Number of Defects
8am-4pm	27
4pm-midnight	35
midnight-8am	49

Test the hypothesis at the .01 level that there is a uniform distribution for the number of defects.

10. A survey conducted by *TV Guide* found men control the zapper in 41% of the homes and women in 19%. It's shared in 27% with the rest saying they don't know of don't have a remote control. A random sample was selected and asked who controlled the zapper in their household and the following data was collected. Test the hypothesis that the data fits the distribution from the TV Guide survey. Use $\alpha = .05$.

Who controls	Number
Men	87
Women	41
Shared	52
Don't know or don't have zapper	18
	198

11. In studies of traits of heredity pairs of identical and fraternal twins were assessed for left or right handedness. Records were kept as to whether they were concordant (both left or both right handed) or not conconcordant (one left and the other right handed.) The data were:

Twin type	both the same	different
Identical	107	28
Fraternal	406	121

At the .01 level, test the hypothesis that the proportion of concordance for the handedness trait is the same for both types of twins.

12. *The American Journal of Economics and Sociology* reports that 1.1 percent of single mothers are under 18 years of age, 16.5 percent are age 18 to 24, 40.2 percent are 25 to 34, 31.6 percent are 35 to 44 and 10.6 percent are 45 or more. A random sample of single mothers yielded the following data:

Age	Number
Under 18	15
18-24	35
25-34	47
35-44	27
45 or more	11

Does the distribution fit the one in the report? Use the .01 level of significance?

13. In clinical trials patients discontinued using NORVASC due to adverse effects. Test the hypothesis that type of adverse effect and dosage are independent variables. Use $\alpha = .01$

Adverse Event	Five mg.	Ten mg.	placebo
Edema	9	29	5
Dizziness	10	9	9
Flushing or palpitation	8	19	5

14. In Dec. 1992, 34 percent thought the economy was improving, 16 percent thought it was getting worse and 48 percent thought it was staying the same. In a nationwide telephone poll conducted by *USA Today*/CNN and Gallup, the following responses were reported:

Prediction	Number
Economy Improving	130
Getting Worse	261
Staying the same	612

Test the hypothesis that there has been no change in opinion between Dec. 1992 and the date of the poll. Use $\alpha = .05$.

15. The following contingency table describes the marital status background of male Vietnam veterans with and without PTSD. Information is from *The Journal of Clinical Psychology*

Marital Status	no PTSD	PTSD
Married	678	200
Living as married	45	44
Separated	9	27
Divorced Widowed	97	17
Never married	42	31

Test the hypothesis that whether or not a male Vietnam vet has PTSD is independent of his marital status. $\alpha = .05$.

16. In order to meet the needs of a large Hispanic population, a school district in Southern Arizona has its students take the Language Assessment Scales (LAS) Test to determine the dominant reading language. The results for first and second grade follow. In this school for the first and second grades is the

primary reading language independent of grade? $\alpha = .01$ *Journal of Educational Issues of Language*

Grade	Spanish reading	English reading
First	242	293
Second	295	362

17. The following data consists of criteria for appropriateness of hospital admission met by inpatients and outpatients with measles, Children's Hospital of Wisconsin during an eight month period of time. Test the hypothesis that the status of inpatient/outpatient is independent of the criteria for admission. Use $\alpha = .05$.

Criteria for admission	inpatients	outpatients
Physiciologic instability	128	88
Dehydration	103	26
Severe Complication	100	7
Meets more than 1 criteria	196	113

18. According to geneticists, in the general population, the distribution of blood type is: 42 percent Type A , 10 percent Type B , 3 percent Type AB, and 45 percent Type O . In 1919 a study of the four blood groups was conducted for various populations. In a group of 116 residents of 18 villages on

Bougainville Island it was observed 74 were type A, 19 type O, 12 type B and 11 type AB. Does the distribution on Bougainville Island fit that of the general population? Use $\alpha = .01$.

Going Beyond

Minitab does not have a Goodness of fit command. Write a macro that will perform a Goodness-of-fit test for a worksheet that has the observed values listed in C1 and the hypothesized percents in C2. Include documentation with # (comments not displayed on the screen) and Note (comments that are displayed on the screen).

13. Regression and Correlation

In this chapter you'll explore how to use MINITAB to explore relationships between two or more quantitative variables.

When you have finished this chapter you should be able to :

- Construct a scatter plot.
- Determine a regression equation.
- Predict values for the response variable with a regression equation.
- Plot the regression line.
- Explain the concepts of residual, standard residuals and fits.
- Construct a multiple regression model.

Simple linear regression analysis is the study of the straight line relationship that exists between two variable. A scatter plot can help determine the pattern of the relationship and give an indication of whether there is a positive linear relationship, a negative one or perhaps no linear relationship. The regression equation will enable us to predict a value for the response variable when a value of the explanatory variable is specified. The correlation coefficient , the coefficient of determination and the standard error of estimate indicate the strength of this relationship.

CONSTRUCTING A SCATTER PLOT

★ **Example:** The number of drinks consumed (x) and the corresponding blood alcohol concentrations (y) are listed for various subjects with the same body weight.

	Drinks	BAC		Drinks	BAC
1	2	0.05	11	3	0.07
2	2	0.07	12	6	0.16
3	4	0.10	13	2	0.06
4	5	0.13	14	4	0.07
5	1	0.01	15	5	0.11
6	4	0.06	16	3	0.08
7	3	0.09	17	2	0.10
8	6	0.15	18	1	0.03
9	7	0.14	19	8	0.19
10	8	0.22	20	6	0.13

a) Enter the data into C1 'drinks' and C2 'BAC'. Produce a scatter plot using 'BAC' as the response variable and 'drinks' as the explanatory (predictor).

b). Based on the scatter plot, do you think there is a A) positive, B) negative or C) no correlation between 'drinks' and 'BAC''?.

c) Based on the scatter plot, do you think there is a A) very strong B) moderately strong or C) weak correlation between 'drinks and BAC'.

★ **Solution:** Once the data is entered, point to the Graph menu and...

Macintosh

Choose **Scatter Plot**. Select 'BAC' for the **Vertical** axis and 'drinks' for the **horizontal**. To print, select **Print**

DOS

Choose **Scatter Plot.** Select 'BAC' for the **Vertical** axis and 'drinks' for the **horizontal** axis. To print, type P.

Windows

Choose **Plot**. Select 'BAC' for Y and 'drinks' for X. To print, select **Print Window** from the File menu.

file from the

File menu.

Your scatter plot should resemble the one shown Note that as the values of x increase, the values of y also increase. The plot indicates that there is a moderately strong positive relationship between the number of years at the company and the width of the office of the employee.

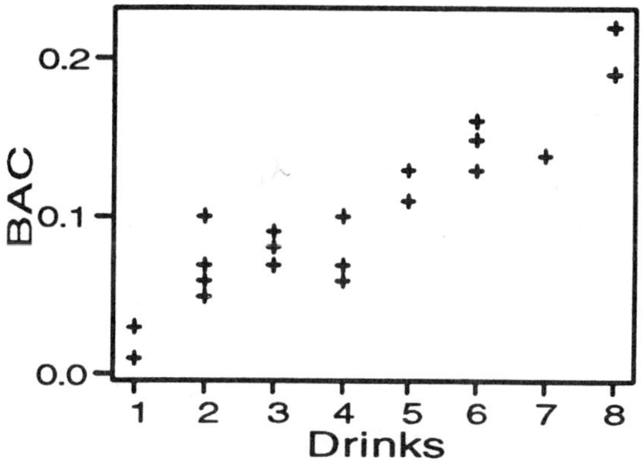

Use a pencil and draw a line that you feel best approximates the pattern of the data. In the next section, we'll examine how to determine the equation of the line that actually does "best-fit" the scatter plot.

DETERMINING THE REGRESSION EQUATION

★ **Example:** Write the regression equation for the BAC data.

★ **Solution:** Choose Regression and then choose Regression again from the Stat menu. Select 'BAC' for the response variable and 'drinks' for the explanatory variable. Your Session window should resemble:

```
MTB > Regress 'BAC' 1 'Drinks'.

The regression equation is
```

```
BAC = 0.0091 + 0.0224 Drinks

Predictor        Coef        Stdev     t-ratio       p
Constant      0.00908      0.01008        0.90   0.379
Drinks       0.022418     0.002179       10.29   0.000

s = 0.02087      R-sq = 85.5%      R-sq(adj) = 84.7%

Unusual Observations
Obs. Drinks BAC  Fit       Stdev.Fit  Residual St.Resid
17   2.00   0.10 0.05392   0.00654    0.04608    2.32R

R denotes an obs. with a large st. resid.
```

The first line indicates the Session window command. The regression equation is equivalent to y = 0.0091 + 0.0224 x

The slope of the line is .0224 which means that each additional drink results in an increase of the BAC of .0224. The Y-intercepts for the line is .0091.

PREDICTING VALUES

The primary purpose of the regression line is to predict values of the response variable using specified values of the explanatory variable.

★ **Example:**

a) Predict the BAC of a person who has had 6 drinks.

b) Predict the BAC of a person who has had 3 drinks.

★ **Solution:** a) Substitute the x value of 6 in the regression equation

BAC = 0.0091 + 0.0224 Drinks

BAC = 0.0091 + 0.0224 (6) = .1435

b) BAC = 0.0091 + 0.0224 (3)= .0763

Examine the Regression output. In addition to the formula for the line or regression, MINITAB outputs information about how dependable the estimate from the prediction equation is likely to be. The standard error of estimate s = .9476 is included to give information about the spread of the data about the regression line.

The coefficient of correlation tells the percent of variation in the response variable that can be explained by the variation is the explanatory variable. `R-sq = 85.5 so 85.5%` of the variation in BAC can be attributed to or explained by the variation in the number of drinks. The remaining 14.5% is unexplained and can be due to other factors (a person's metabolism rate, how much they have eaten etc.) or random sampling error.

Most of the other output contains information needed to perform a hypothesis test about how dependable the regression line model is.

Let's return to the regression dialog box and examine the storage options. Select St. Residuals, Residuals, Fits and Coefficients.

```
MTB > Name c3= 'SRES1'c4 ='FITS1'c5 ='RESI1'c6= 'COEF1'
MTB > Regress 'BAC' 1 'Drinks';
SUBC>   SResiduals 'SRES1';
SUBC>   Fits 'FITS1';
SUBC>   Residuals 'RESI1';
SUBC>   Coefficients 'COEF1'.

The regression equation is
BAC = 0.0091 + 0.0224 Drinks
```

	Drinks	BAC	SRES1	FITS1	RESI1	COEF1
1	2	0.05	-0.19781	0.053922	-0.0039216	0.0090850
2	2	0.07	0.81104	0.053922	0.0160784	0.0224183
3	4	0.10	0.06104	0.098758	0.0012418	
4	5	0.13	0.43571	0.121176	0.0088235	
5	1	0.01	-1.12043	0.031503	-0.0215033	
6	4	0.06	-1.90510	0.098758	-0.0387582	
7	3	0.09	0.67611	0.076340	0.0136601	
8	6	0.15	0.32155	0.143595	0.0064052	
9	7	0.14	-1.34506	0.166013	-0.0260131	
10	8	0.22	1.70766	0.188431	0.0315686	
11	3	0.07	-0.31379	0.076340	-0.0063399	
12	6	0.16	0.82355	0.143595	0.0164052	
13	2	0.06	0.30661	0.053922	0.0060784	
14	4	0.07	-1.41356	0.098758	-0.0287582	
15	5	0.11	-0.55190	0.121176	-0.0111765	
16	3	0.08	0.18116	0.076340	0.0036601	
17	2	0.10	2.32432	0.053922	0.0460784	
18	1	0.03	-0.07833	0.031503	-0.0015033	
19	8	0.19	0.08485	0.188431	0.0015686	
20	6	0.13	-0.68247	0.143595	-0.0135948	

The last column, 'Coeff1' lists in the y-intercept and the slope for the equation. (In this case: `BAC = 0.0090850 + 0.0224183 Drinks`)

When you predicted the BAC for a person who has had 6 drinks, you computed `BAC = 0.0091 + 0.0224 (6) = .1435.` The coefficients given in the Data window have a greater degree of accuracy and using them for the prediction would give:

`BAC = 0.0090850 + 0.0224183 (6)= .1435948.` Now compare this result to the one underlined in the output in the Fits1 column in row 8. You can probably guess that the Fits column is the value predicted for y when the value for x in the same row is substituted in the regression equation. Use a calculator to confirm the entry in the Fits column for row 1 is the result of substituting $x = 2$ in the regression equation.

The *residual* for each row is the difference between the y data value (BAC) and the y value in the Fits column. Thus, for the first row, verify that

`0.05 - 0.053922 = -0.0039216` (error due to round off)

The SRes column reports the residual as a standard z-score and can alert you to any unusual values. As you know, 99.7% of these values will fall between -3 and 3. A value that is greater than 2 or less than -2 is considered to be an unusual value since these values will only occur 5% of the time. Note that MINITAB reports as an unusual occurrence the entries in row 17 since the SRes is 2.32. It's a good practice to examine the rows on which these outliers occur to look reasons for the unusual occurrences or for possible data entry errors.

PLOTTING THE REGRESSION LINE

Let's now see how to construct the regression line on our scatter plot. To do so, select the Graph menu and ...

Macintosh

Choose **Scatter Plot**. Select 'years' for the **Vertical** axis and 'width' for the **horizontal** axis. To connect the points, use the **Lines** option. Select 'years' for the **Y column** and 'width' for the **X column.** To print, select **Print file**

DOS

Choose **Scatter Plot**. Select 'years' for the **Vertical** axis and 'width' for the **horizontal** axis. To connect the points, use the **Lines** option. Select 'years' for the **Y column** and 'width' for the **X column.** To print, type P.

Windows

Choose **Plot**. Select 'years' for **Y** and 'width' for **X.** Use the **annotation** pull down menu and select **Line**. Type two coordinate pairs to define the endpoints. Type 1 .03150 8 .188431. Choose the **multiple graphs** option and select from the **File** menu.

Overlay on same page.

Let's now examine the graph of the line of regression. Use the Describe command to find the mean of 'drinks' the mean 'BAC'. The graph of the regression will always pass through the point $(\overline{x}, \overline{y})$.

Each point on the scatter plot represents a data point. Each point on the line has a y coordinate corresponding to the predicted value for the given x. These values are, of course, found in the Fits column. The residual is the difference between the y value of the data point and the y value on the line. When the residual is positive, the point will lie above the regression line and when the residual is negative, the points will fall below the line.

★ **Example:**

a) Locate the point $(\overline{x}, \overline{y})$ on the graph .
b) Locate the point corresponding to the data point in row 17 having coordinates (2, .10)
c) Locate the point on the line with x = 2, y = .053922 (the Fits value).
d) Discuss the significance of the residual for this row.

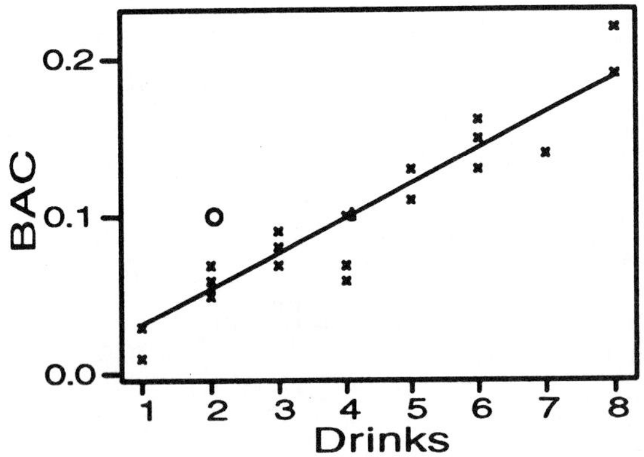

★ **Solution:**

a) The point $(\overline{x}, \overline{y})$ is on the line of regression marked with a solid triangle.
b) The data point is marked with a circle.
c) The Fits point is on the line marked with a triangle.
d) The residual is positive since the data point is above the line. The data point is a distance of .0460784 above the line.

THE CORRELATION COEFFICIENT

To find the correlation coefficient, choose Basic Statistics and then Correlation from the **Stat** menu. Select as many variables as you wish. Minitab will create a matrix in which each variable is correlated with each other chosen variable.

★ **Example:** Find the correlation coefficient for 'drinks' and 'BAC'.

★ **Solution:** Select the two variable in the correlation command. The Session window will report:

```
MTB > Correlation 'Drinks' 'BAC'.

Correlation of Drinks and BAC = 0.925

MTB >
```

MULTIPLE REGRESSION

In simple regression analysis there are two variables and on is designated as the explanatory variable and the other as the response. Often a more accurate model can be developed using several explanatory variables for the one response variable.

★ **Example:** Before hiring new employees, the personnel director for Worldwide Things, Inc, decides to do a regression analysis of the company's current salary structure. She believes that an employee's salary is related to the number of years of work experience (YEARS) and to the number of years of post-high school education (POSTHSED). The data for this study can be found on '13Data.MTW'.

a) Develop the regression equation. What is the constant? What are the coefficients?

b) What is the Standard error of estimate?
c) What is the coefficient of determination? Interpret this value in the context of the problem.
d) Predict a salary for an employee with no experience and no post high-school education.
e) Predict a salary for an employee with 6 years of work experience and 4 years of post-high school education.
f) Find the correlation between the variables in pairs.
g) What is the Fits value for the data in row 6? Show how this value is computed.
h) What is the Residual in row 6. Show how it relates to the Fits value?

★ **Solution:** Choose **Regression** and then choose **Regression** again from the Stat menu. Choose 'YEARS' and 'POSTHSED' for the **predictors** and choose 'SALARY' for the **response variable**. Click on the options for Residuals, Standard residuals, Fits and Coefficients. The following output will be found in the Session window.

```
    The regression equation is
    SALARY = 26943 + 705 YEARS + 559 POSTHSED

Predictor         Coef        Stdev     t-ratio       p
Constant       26942.5        765.1       35.22   0.000
YEARS            705.4        104.8        6.73   0.000
POSTHSED         558.7        332.8        1.68   0.095

s = 4882          R-sq = 72.8%       R-sq(adj) = 72.4%

MTB > Correlation 'SALARY' 'POSTHSED' 'YEARS'.

          SALARY POSTHSED
POSTHSED   0.803
YEARS      0.850    0.909

MTB >
```

a) The regression equation is `SALARY = 26943 + 705 YEARS + 559 POSTHSED`. The constant is 26943, the coefficient for 'YEARS' is 705 and the coefficient for 'POSTHSED' is 559. For each additional year at the company (when the education level is held constant) an employee will get $705. For each additional year of education (when the years at the company is held constant) the employee will get an additional $559.

b) The Standard error of estimate is `s = 4882.`

c) The coefficient of determination is R-sq = 72.8%. This means 72.8 percent of the variation in salary at Worldwide can be attributed to variation in the number of years at the company and the level of post high school education. 27.2 percent is unexplained by these variables and may be due to other factors such as performance level.

d) The salary for person with no post high school education and no years experience would be predicted as $26,943.

SALARY = 26943 + 705 (0)+ 559 (0) = 26943. Note that this is the constant term in the equation.

e)The salary for a person with 6 years experience and 4 years of post high school education would be predicted as `SALARY = 26943 + 705 (6)+ 559 (4)`= $33,409.

f) There is a .803 correlation between 'SALARY' and 'POSTHSED' . The correlation between 'YEARS' and 'SALARY' is .850 and the correlation between 'YEARS' and 'POSTHSED' is .909.

g) The value of Fits in row 6 is $30881.30. It is computed from `SALARY = 26943 + 705 (4)+ 559 (2)`= $30,881.30

h) The residual in row 6 is $-3338.30. Salary -Fits = 27543 - 30881.30 = -3338.3. Note that the corresponding point falls below the regression line.

Exercises

Answer all questions in paragraph form.

1. Enter the following data into a Minitab worksheet.

x	0	1	2	3	4	5	6	7
y	1	3	5	7	9	11	13	15

   a. Construct a scatter plot for the variables. Describe the relationship.
   b. Calculate the formula for the line of regression using Minitab. Let y be the response variable and x the predictor. What is the slope? What is the y-intercept?
   c. Calculate the correlation coefficient.
   d. Predict a value for y when x= 8. Now use the regression equation to predict the value.
   e. Exchange the roles of x and y and calculate a regression equation. That is, use x for the response variable and y for the predictor. Is your answer the same as in a? Construct a scatter plot for this line (use x for the vertical axis and y for the horizontal.)
   f. Most regression problems are *not* of this sort. Write a brief paragraph explaining the findings of this problem, discussing why this one is different. Explain how the slope and the y-intercept could be computed without Minitab. Discuss the value of the correlation coefficient.

2. Enter the following data into a Minitab worksheet.

x	0	1	2	3	4	5	6	7
y	23	20	17	14	11	8	5	2

a. Construct a scatter plot for the variables. Describe the relationship.
b. Calculate the formula for the line of regression using Minitab. Let y be the response variable and x the predictor.
c. Calculate the correlation coefficient.
d. Predict a value for y when x= 8. Now use the regression equation to predict the value.
e. Exchange the roles of x and y and calculate a regression equation. That is, use x for the response variable and y for the predictor. Is your answer the same as in a? Construct a scatter plot for this line.

For problems 3 to 11:

a) Construct a scatter plot and decide whether there is an indication of a positive correlation, a negative correlation or no correlation.

b) Calculate the equation for the line of regression. Use the Standard Residuals, the Residuals, the fits and the coefficients options.

c) Find the standard error of estimate.

d) What is the coefficient of determination. Interpret this value in the context of the given data.

e) For each problem a value is given for x. Use the regression equation to predict a value for y.

f) Examine row 3 of your Data window. What is the value in the Fits column? What is the value in the Residual column? Explain the relationship by using numerical values.

g) Are there any unusual data points? Why or why not?

h) Use the Correlation command and calculate the correlation coefficient.

3. Kelly Sanchez is a college senior interviewing at several companies for a management position. When she tours the offices at ADT Corp. she thinks she notices some are a great deal more spacious than others and wonders if there is a relationship between the number of years at the company and the length of the office. A random sample produced the following data pairs:

x = no. of years at a company y = width of office space (feet)

x	3	16	7	4	15	7	8	5
y	4	40	16	9	38	16	17	10

Predict the office space (y) for a person who has been at the company 10 years. (x = 10).

4. Mark Z. Papers is a 6th grade teacher who feels there is a relationship between his student's I.Q. scores and the hours they watch television each week. The following represent a sample of his data.

Test y = 6th grader's IQ score y = hours watching TV per week

x	125	116	97	114	85	107	105
y	5	14	30	16	41	25	21

Predict the number of hours watched per week from a 6th grader with an IQ score of 108.

5. Douglas Michaels, a pre-med student, wants to determine if there is a relationship between the age of a youngster and the number of doctor visits they make in a year. He has collected the following data from a random sample:

x = age and y = number of doctor visits last year.

x	5	6	8	14	15	7	8	12
y	9	2	12	17	9	16	6	15

Predict the number of doctor visits for a 7 year old.

6. In a study of autistic children, clinical characteristics were measured. A Psychologist wants to determine whether there is a linear relationship between the behavioral score (the total score on a test of 29 items; 0 = absence of symptoms and 116 = maximum severity and y = language score (on a scale of 1 to 5 where 1 = absence of signs or normal development and 5 = maximum severity of signs or severe retardation. The following data appeared in *The American Journal of Psychiatry*, July 1992.

Behavior	Language
27	2
35	4
65	4
67	4
47	3
46	3
63	4
44	4
34	5
51	4
17	2

Behavior	Language
40	2
41	4
60	5
24	5
48	4
29	2
73	5
60	3
41	4
27	3

Predict a behavior score for a student with a language score of 48.

7. Castle Rock Entertainment produced many movies over the past few years. On of the vice-presidents wants to see if there is a relationship between the total

cost of the film (including marketing as well as production and salaries.) and Gross income for ticket sales in American movie theaters. Source: Castle Rock Entertainment.

Cost $million	Gross Income $million	Cost $million	Gross Income $million
55	150.5	26	5.0
42	123.0	19	10.0
17	68.0	35	35.0
30	93.0	22	20.0
43	16.0	13	15.0

Predict the gross income when the cost is $40 million.

8. The Buffalo Bills and the Dallas Cowboys were the two Super Bowl teams for 1993. The following represents the number of games each team won in the indicated season.

Year	Bills	Cowboys	Year	Bills	Cowboys
1983	5	9	1989	13	3
1984	8	12	1990	9	1
1985	2	9	1991	15	7
1986	2	10	1992	15	11
1987	4	7	1993	14	15
1988	7	7			

Predict y when x = 6.

9. The Rip-Off Vending Machine Company operates coffee vending machines in several office buildings. The company wants to study the relationship, if any, which exists between the number of cups of coffee sold per day and the number of persons working in each building. Data for this study were collected by the company and are presented below:

Cups	Persons	Cups	Persons	Cups	Persons
5	10	19	40	18	40
6	20	15	30	22	40
14	30	11	20	26	50

Predict y when x is 12 cups.

10. A regional development council, composed of members from several local chambers of commerce, gathered the following data from selected firms in the region that produced similar products.

Cost $thousands	Output	Cost $thousands	Output
150	40	162	75
140	38	180	70
160	48	165	90
170	56	190	110
150	62	185	120

Predict the output when the cost is $145 thousand.

11. Katie Dvorak trains employees to use a specific statistical software package. Selected trainees have turned in the following performances in recent weeks.

Trainee	Hours of Training	Errors
A	1	6
B	4	3
C	6	2
D	8	1
E	2	5
F	3	1
G	1	7

Predict the number of errors for a person with 5 hours of training.

12. *The American Journal of Psychiatry* recently published an article describing an investigation of cortical brain dysfunction and its relationship to infantile autism. Twenty -one children received extensive evaluation including a behavioral score (on a scale 1-116), a language score (on a scale of 1-5), a neurological score (a scale of 1 to 5) and a measurement of the mean cortical cerebral blood flow CBF (ml/100g/min). The data are in '13mreg.MTW'.

   a. Use behavior, language and neurologic as predictors and CBF as the response variable and produce a regression equation.

   b. Predict a CBF value for an autistic child with a behavioral score of 45, a language score of 4 and a neurological score of 2.

   c. Predict a CBF value for an autistic child with a behavioral score of 67, a language score of 2 and a neurological score of 1.

   d. Interpret the Behavior coefficient.

   e. Interpret the Language coefficient.

   f. What is the coefficient of determination?

   g. Interpret the coefficient of determination in the context of this problem.

   h. What is the standard error of estimate?

13. Use the data from the previous problem and designate language as the response variable and behavior, CBF and neurologic as the predictors. Repeat steps a to h from problem 12.

14. Nonparametric Statistics

The assumptions (such as normality or equal variances) about populations can often not be verified. In this chapter we will present alternate techniques for testing hypotheses about such populations. Unlike parametric tests, nonparametric tests are useful for ordinal data as well as interval and ratio data.

When you have completed this chapter you should be able to:

- Conduct a Sign test to determine if there is a difference between pairs of data.
- Conduct a Wilcoxon Sign test for the difference between data pairs.
- Conduct a Mann-Whitney (U) test.
- Conduct a Kruskal-Wallis test.
- Conduct a Runs test for randomness
- Compute the Spearman rank correlation coefficient.

CONDUCTING A SIGN TEST

A sign test is used to compare sample means from two samples that are not independent such as in a before-and-after test. The difference of the two measures is computed, but only the *sign* of the difference is used. The *amount* of the difference is disregarded.

★ **Example:** A work-out area and a swimming pool were installed at the site of a large corporation in an effort to lower the body mass index (BMI) of participating employees and thus lower the company's group insurance rates. Each participant's BMI was measured at the start to determine a baseline value. After two years in the program, the BMI of each participant was measured again. The data for a random sample of 16 participating employees are found in

'14data.MTW'. Use a sign test at the .05 level to see if there has been a decrease in BMI in the two-year period.

★ **Solution:** The hypotheses are:

H_0: The proportion of positive signs is .5. (Half the differences are above the median and hence half are below).

H_1: The proportion of positive signs is less than .5. (There are more negative differences).

To perform a sign test, construct a new column 'diff'. Use the Let command to find the difference between 'Two-year' and 'Baseline'.

```
MTB > Name c3 = 'Diff'
MTB > Let 'Diff' = 'Two-year'- 'Baseline'
```

Naturally when the difference is negative the 'Baseline' value is above, when the difference is positive, the 'Two-year' value is below and when the difference is zero, the values are equal and there has been no change.

Choose **Nonparametric** and then **One-Sample sign** from the Stat menu. Select 'Diff' for the variable. Choose the **Test median** option and choose the alternative hypothesis of **Less Than** from the drop down menu.

```
MTB > STest 0.0 'Diff';
SUBC>   Alternative -1.
```

The Session window will report the results of the left tail (L.T.) sign test.

```
SIGN TEST OF MEDIAN = 0.00000 VERSUS  L.T.  0.00000

        N  BELOW  EQUAL  ABOVE   P-VALUE     MEDIAN
Diff   16      6      1      9    0.8491    0.03500
```

From your data window, it's easy to verify that there are 6 negative signs, 9 positive and 1 one zero entry in the 'diff' column. The p-value for this test is .8491 indicating the null hypothesis should not be rejected. There is not enough evidence to say there is a difference after two-years.
Note that if the null hypothesis is true, i.e. the median is 0, the proportion of positive differences will be .5 indicating half the values will be greater than 0 and the proportion of negative differences will be .5, so half the signs will be negative.

CONDUCTING A WILCOXON SIGNED RANK TEST

A Wilcoxon signed rank test uses the magnitude of the difference between two variables as well as the sign of the difference to see if there are true differences between the pairs of data.

★ **Example:** To illustrate this test, we'll use the BMI example again. Now let's make a decision based on the *amount* of BMI change and not just the direction.

★ **Solution:** The hypotheses are:
H_0: The BMI values are equal.
H_1: There has been a change in the BMI values.

Choose **Nonparametric** and then **One-Sample Wilcoxon** from the Stat menu. Just as in the Sign test, select 'Diff' for the variable. Choose the **Test median** option and use the default alternative as **Not Equal.**

```
MTB > WTest 0.0 'Diff';
SUBC>   Alternative 0.
```

The Session window output is as follows:

```
TEST OF MEDIAN = 0.000000 VERSUS MEDIAN N.E. 0.000000
```

```
        FOR          WILCOXON                    ESTIMATED
        N    TEST   STATISTIC   P-VALUE           MEDIAN
Diff    16    15        60.0      1.000       0.007500
MTB >
```

Since one of the pairs had a zero difference, there were 15 pairs used for this test. The Wilcoxon T statistic is 60. The p-value is 1, indicating the null hypothesis should be accepted. (It's virtually impossible that the alternative hypothesis is true.)

CONDUCTING A MANN-WHITNEY TEST

A Mann-Whitney test is appropriate to use to test for differences between two sets of data when the data are drawn from independent samples and the populations are not normally distributed.

★ **Example:** Scores on individual measures on the Wide Range Achievement Test (WRAT reading subtest) are given for chronic schizophrenic patients and normal comparison subjects. Test the hypothesis that there is no difference at the .05 level in the WRAT scores of the two groups. The data for this test are found in 'Experiml' and 'Control' of '14data.MTW.'

★ **Solution:** The hypotheses are:
H_0: The WRAT scores of the two groups are equal.
H_1: The WRAT scores of the groups are not equal..

Choose **Nonparametric** and then **Mann-Whitney** from the **Stat** menu. Select 'Experiml" for the First Sample and 'Control' for the Second Sample. Since the test is at the .05 level, select the 95% confidence level. Use the default NE (not equal) alternative hypothesis.

```
MTB > Mann-Whitney 95.0 'Experiml' 'Control';
SUBC>   Alternative 0.
```

The Session window will report the results of the test:

```
Mann-Whitney Confidence Interval and Test

experiml    N =  13      Median =        90.00
control     N =  17      Median =       106.00
Point estimate for ETA1-ETA2 is         -15.00
95.1 Percent C.I. for ETA1-ETA2 is (-21.00,-7.00)
W = 116.0
Test of ETA1=ETA2 vs. ETA1≠ETA2 is significant at .0004
The test is significant at 0.0004 (adjusted for ties)
```

The output contains the number in each sample and the median for each sample. A point estimate and an interval estimate are made for the value of the difference in the medians (ETA1 -ETA2). Since this interval does not contain 0, it's likely that the null hypothesis should be rejected. This is confirmed by the p-value which is .0004. At the .05 level, reject the null hypothesis and conclude that there is a difference in the WRAT scores of the two groups.

CONDUCTING A KRUSKAL-WALLIS TEST

A Kruskal-Wallis test is appropriate to use when testing the difference among three or more populations and the conditions for analysis of variance can not be met.

★ **Example:** In a test to determine whether mental skills are different for different age groups subjects in their 30's, 50's, 60's and 70's were given a 'digits backward' test in which a psychologist reads a sequence of digits and the subject is asked to recite them in reverse order. The data, found in 'thirties', 'fifties', sixties' and seventies' of '14data.MTW' represents the number of digits correctly recited for each. Use a Kruskal-Wallis test to test the hypothesis that the means for all four age groups are equal at the .01 level of significance.

★ **Solution:** The hypotheses are:

H_0: The scores of the groups are equal.
H_1: The scores in at least one of the groups are not equal to the others.

To perform the K-W test, the data must be in a single column with a second column designating the group (factor). Use the **Stack** command to stack all scores in 'Digits'. Select the **subscript** option and **Store** them in 'Decade'.

```
MTB > Name c10 = 'Digits' c11 = 'Decade'
MTB > Stack ('Thirties') ( 'Fifties') ('Sixties')
('Sevent') ('Digits');
SUBC>   Subscripts 'Decade'.
```

Choose **Nonparametric** and then **Kruskal-Wallis** from the Stat menu. Choose 'Digits' as the response variable and 'Decade' for the Factor. The Session window output will be:

```
MTB > Kruskal-Wallis 'Digits' 'Decade'.

LEVEL      NOBS    MEDIAN  AVE. RANK   Z VALUE
    1         9     6.000       18.6      0.80
    2         9     5.000       15.2     -0.50
    3         7     7.000       17.9      0.46
    4         7     5.000       14.1     -0.77
OVERALL      32                 16.5

H = 1.27  d.f. = 3  p = 0.737
H = 1.34  d.f. = 3  p = 0.719 (adjusted for ties)
```

For each group (level), the number of observation (NOBS), the median, the average rank and the z-value is reported. The chi-square distribution used has 4-1 =3 degrees of freedom. The test statistic, H = 1.27 has a high p-value of .737 indicating that the null hypothesis should be accepted. (.737 > .05) There is no significant difference among the age groups.

CONDUCTING A RUNS TEST FOR RANDOMNESS

The runs test is used to determine if there is a pattern in the behavior of data.

★ **Example:** Anna Liszt, a stock broker is keeping track of a particular stock and keeps a daily record of increases and decreases for a period of 100 days. The data are recorded in 'UpOrDown' of '14data.MTW'. Use a runs test to determine if there is a pattern in the sequence of the data.

★ **Solution:** H_0: There is no underlying pattern in the data.
H_1: There is an underlying pattern in the data.
The given data is in alpha form and the data for a runs test must be in a numeric column , so the first task is to convert the given data into numeric form. This task could be done manually, but let's do the job with MINITAB.

MINITAB's convert command requires four columns.

1. A column for the original data (the original is the alpha data.)
2. A column for the converted data (numeric).

A conversion table must be set up in two additional columns.

3. A column containing every possible original value
4. A column with the converted values. These will be the numeric values.

In most cases you will be converting from alpha to numeric data, however, the Convert command will also convert from numeric to alpha-just reverse the pairs of entries in the dialog box.

The table, consisting of the last two columns should be:

ROW	original	convert
1	U	1
2	D	-1
3	0	0

Hint: Be careful this command is case sensitive and interprets D differently from d.

To convert the values from alpha to numeric, choose the **Convert** command from the following menu:

For the **Input data** column, select the column that contains the data you want to convert, in our case it's 'UpOrDown'. Next, for the **Output data** specify 'Runstest' as the column to store the **converted data**. For the Conversion Table select 'UpOrDown', the values you want to convert, for the Original. and for the Converted, select the column that contains the second part of the conversion table (that is, the codes you will use to represent the original data).

```
MTB > Name c15 = 'Runstest'
MTB > Convert 'original' 'convert' 'UpOrDown'
'Runstest'.
```

For the test, choose **Nonparametric** and then **Runs** from the Stat menu. Choose 'Runstest' for the variable. The Session window output will be:

```
MTB > Runs 'Runstest'.
    Runstest

    K =      -0.0600

    The observed no. of runs =   42
    The expected no. of runs =   50.9800
    49 Observations above K   51 below

              The test is significant at  0.0712
              Cannot reject at alpha = 0.05
```

The Session window clearly tells it all. Accept the null hypothesis and conclude that there is no pattern in the data.

COMPUTING THE SPEARMAN RANK CORRELATION COEFFICIENT

The Spearman rank correlation coefficient measures the degree of relationship between ordinal or ranked data. When actual values of x and y are given, use the Pearson Product-Moment correlation coefficient discussed in the chapter on regression in your text.

★ **Example:** Three management trainee positions are open at a large retail chain. Eight candidates are being considered for the jobs. The marketing director and a the vice president will make the final hiring decision. They each rank the eight applicants in order of preference where 1 = first choice and 8 = last choice. The rankings are as listed in 'MD rank' and 'VP rank' of '14data.MTW'. Compute the Spearman rank correlation coefficient.

★ **Solution:** Select Basic Statistics and Correlation from the Stat menu. Select 'MD rank' and 'VP rank' as the variables. The output will appear in your Session window.

```
MTB > Correlation 'MD rank' 'VP rank'.

Correlation of MD rank and VP rank = 0.892
```

The Spearman rank correlation coefficient is .892. There is a positive correlation in the rankings of the two executives.

If you need to compute the Spearman rank correlation coefficient and the actual value of the variables is given, you can simply use the Rank command to produce the required form for the data.

*Notes*____

Exercises

1. In preliminary tests to determine whether or not to continue research and development of the effectiveness of Efichol a new drug designed to lower cholesterol levels, a pharmaceutical company tests the cholesterol level of ten people before and after a six week clinical trial of the new drug. The data are in C1 '1before' and C2 '1after'. Use a sign test of paired differences to test the effectiveness of the medicine at the .05 level.

2. The pharmaceutical company is now interested in doing more detailed tests for the effectiveness of the drug. For the data in problem 1, use a Wilcoxon sign test to test the effectiveness of the medicine at the .05 level.

3. Sonny Schein, a meteorologist, wants to determine if there is a pattern in the average daily temperature and keeps records of increases (+), decreases (-) and no change (0) in temperature for month of July. The data are in C3 'Sonny'. Conduct a runs test for randomness at the .05 level of significance.

4. It has been estimated that 80% of all lower back pain cases are caused by weak trunk muscles. Studies have suggested that improved strength of the trunk muscles will aid in the prevention and treatment of lower back pain. In a study to compare the effect of various training frequencies on the development of strength participants were randomly assigned to one of four groups. Training group 1 = once every other week. Training group 2 = once a week. Training group 3 = twice a week and Training group 4 = three times a week. The data in C4- C7 'Group 1' 'Group 2' 'Group 3' and 'Group 4' represents the weight (kg) for each of the participants at the beginning of the program. Use a Kruskal-Wallis test to test the hypothesis that the mean weights of the four groups are equal. Let α =.05. *Physical Therapy*

5. *Psychology Today* recently published the results of a study to determine if there was a relationship between a city's characteristic pace and its rate of

coronary heart disease. As a simple measure of concern with clock time they counted the percentage of men and women who were wearing watches and ranked the cities from highest percent = 1 to lowest. They also ranked each of these cities for the rate of CHD. The data are in C8-A, C9 and C10, 'City' 'Watches' and 'CHD'. Compute the Spearman rank correlation coefficient.

6. In a study to measure neuropsychological functioning for chronic schizophrenic patients and normal comparison subjects each participant was given the Benton Visual Retention Test. The number of errors made by individuals in each group is given in C11 'Chrschiz' and C12 'Normal'. Test the hypothesis at the .01 level that the mean number of errors for both groups is the same. *American Journal of Psychiatry*.

7. Polly Esta, owner of Natural Textiles, Ltd. is concerned about the chronically low daily output of her factory workers. Therefore, she has devised a bonus plan and wants to found out if this bonus plan will result in any improvement. (She is not concerned at this time with the degree of productivity improvement.) Eight workers were offered the bonus plan. Their daily output before and after the bonus plan (in hundreds of units) is given in C14 '7before' and C15 '7after'.Use a sign test to determine if there has been a significant improvement at $\alpha = .05$ after the plan.

8. Now Polly would like to investigate further. Use a Wilcoxon sign test to see if the workers from problem 7 showed improvement after the bonus plan was introduced. Use $\alpha = .05$.

9. A record of the first digit in the daily number drawing is given in C16 'number'. Test to see if there is a pattern of odd and even digits by conducting a runs test for the randomness.

10. Language comprehension appears to decrease with advancing age. In a study to determine which factors contribute significantly to comprehension difficulty, paid volunteers who were recruited through advertising in local

newspapers had their hearing levels tested. The data in C20-C21 represents the pure-tone average in db HTL for the subjects separated by age group (30's, 50's, 60's and 70's.) Test the hypothesis that the mean level is the same for all age groups. Use the .05 level of significance. *Applied Psycholinguistics*.

11. Transcutaneous electrical nerve stimulation (TENS) devises are frequently used in management of acute and chronic pain conditions. An important component of the TENS system is the skin electrode. A study in *Physical Therapy* was done to determine conductive differences in electrodes used with TENS devises. Eleven devises from a low-impedance group were tested in two different trials. The results (in units of 100 ohms of impedance) are given in C24 and C25, 'Trial 1' and 'Trial 2'. Use the sign test of paired differences to test the hypothesis that the second trial values were higher than those in the first trial. Use the .05 level of significance.

12. For the data in problem 11, use the Wilcoxon sign test to test the hypothesis that the second trial values were higher than those of the first. $\alpha = .05$

13. Six company managers were being evaluated for promotion by two of the companies vice presidents where 1 = the highest ranking. The rankings are given in C26 'VP A' and C27 'VP B'. Compute the Spearman rank correlation coefficient.

14. Executives at Trans Earth Airlines (TEA) are disturbed about numerous passenger complaints concerning late arrivals at Los Angeles Airport (LAX). In order to see if there is a pattern to late arrivals, a record is kept for 40 consecutive flights. (Airlines agree that a plane that arrives within 10 minutes of its scheduled arrival time will be considered to be on time.) The data is in C28-A 'LAX'. (E = early, L = late and O = on time.) Test to determine whether there is a pattern to late arrivals or do the times of arrivals occur randomly. $\alpha = .05$

15. The perceived discount PD is measured by PD = (perceived regular price - perceived sale price)/perceived regular price. A study to determine if the PD for high-image stores will be higher than for that of low-image store was published in *The Journal of Consumer Research*. The data in C32 'AD' C33 'May PD' and C34 'Nordy PD represent values for the perceived discount at various actual discount AD rates at the May Company and at Nordstrom's for name brand items. Use a sign test to test the hypothesis that the Perceived discounts are lower at Nordstrom's than at the May Company. Use the .05 level of significance.

16. Use the Wilcoxon sign test to test the hypothesis that perceived discounts are lower at Nordstrom's than at the May Company. $\alpha = .05$

17. Scores on measures of emotional distress are given in C35 'Smoker' and C36 'Nonsmoke' for nicotine-dependent smokers and nonsmokers. Test the hypothesis at the .01 level that there is no difference in the mean scores for the two groups. *American Journal of Psychiatry*

18. A career counselor claims that there is no difference in career decision-making skills among various ethnic groups. Results of scores on a test to determine career decision-making skills are given in C37-C39. Test the counselor's claim at the .01 level. *Career Development Quarterly*,

19. The new national health care plan to be instituted in the last half of the 1990's requires many more primary care physicians and fewer specialists. The 20 top ranked medical school in research (determined by research funds acquired) have also been ranked for their production of primary care physicians. The paired rankings are found in C40 'Research' and C41'Primary' *1992 Institutional Goals Ranking Report Association of American Medical Colleges*. Compute the Spearman rank correlation coefficient.

20. Seven volunteers try a new liquid diet of *Slender Fast* for two weeks. Their weights before and after are given in C43 'before' and C44 'after'. Use a sign test with $\alpha = .05$ to determine if there is a decrease in weight following the liquid diet.

21. Use the Wilcoxon sign test to test for a significant decrease in weight for the *Slender Fast* volunteers. Use $\alpha = .05$

22. A recent study in the *American Journal of Psychology* involved normal subjects and alcoholics. Some normal subjects and some of the alcoholics were given Lorazepam and some from each group given a placebo. A metabolic measure at the cerebellum (a part of the brain) was then determined (μmol/100 g/min) for each subject. The measures are found in C45-C48 "Nplaccbo', 'Nloraz' 'Aplacebo' and Aloraz'. Test the hypothesis at the .05 level that the metabolic values are equal for all four groups.

23. A second grade teacher wanted to insure that he was calling on girls and on boys in his class in a random pattern. The data are in C49 "boygirl'. Use the runs test for randomness at the .05 level.

24. Ms. Anne Tenna, a first year middle school teacher, claims that television viewing habits are the same for students in different middle school grades. She questioned of a sample of her students about how many minutes they watch television each night and produced the data found in C50-C52, '6th', 7th' and '8th'. Test Ms. Tenna's claim at the .05 level.

25. A government health care official investigated the relationship between the average tax paid by residents of each state and the number of new cancer cases for 1993. The data are in C53-C55, 'State' 'Tax rank' and 'Cancer'. Compute the Spearman rank correlation coefficient.

Index

NOTES

NOTES

NOTES

NOTES

NOTES

NOTES

NOTES

NOTES